To Connor - congra
passing the course. G
You future sales caree. Best wishes,
Matt

CONVERTED
HOW TO HELP MORE PEOPLE BUY WHAT YOU SELL

MATT SYKES

RETHINK PRESS

First published in Great Britain in 2020
by Rethink Press (www.rethinkpress.com)

Contents

This book was written during lockdown in 2020 and is dedicated to the selfless employees of the NHS whose tireless work helped save thousands of lives during the Coronavirus pandemic.

Foreword

What were you hoping that you would discover when you decided to look through these pages?

What success or personal victory are you trying to accomplish?

I was just wondering, because – you know – sales books can be a bit of a gamble, can't they?

Some promise you untold riches, but end up just leaving you a little poorer, while others might look a bit old-fashioned or outdated, and yet offer hidden sales gold.

It can be a bit of a lottery at the best of times.

So, if you are browsing online or standing in a bookstore holding this book, and think to yourself, 'I'll just take a look inside to see whether it's for me' – what is it that you are you hoping for?

I'm really curious.

We're living in an age where people don't just hope for immediate returns on their investment – they demand them.

Some books on this subject are the equivalent of a drive-through, fast food burger lunch. The person who threw it together did so with very little love or care, and although it makes you feel better for a while, none of it has actually done you any good.

Then there are books like this one, where the ingredients have been expertly sourced and when you've finished it, you'll want to share the experience with others. You can tell that every page, in every chapter, matters to the person who wrote it and each piece of advice given has clearly come from over twenty years of experience.

Matt Sykes (the wonderful chap who wrote the rest of this book) has a number of incredibly admirable qualities. First off, he is a genuinely nice guy. He has a great sense of humour, is incredibly generous and is one of those people who light up a room.

But let's turn to his wealth of experience – because nothing in this book is untested theory dressed up to look like fact.

It's practical, brilliant, real-world advice.

Matt Sykes knows what he is talking about because – here's the thing – Matt Sykes has lived all this. He's passionate about sales being seen as a force for good, and throughout his books and keynote speeches, he often uses the words 'help' and 'journey'.

Those two words say so much about his philosophy. He is on a mission to help people who sell – and he wants those people to help their prospects and customers. I'm big on 'help' too – I believe changing the word 'selling' for 'helping' is one of the biggest paradigm shifts that a sales team can make – and has an incredible effect on results.

But equally important is 'journey'. Journey originates from a French word that literally means 'all day'. Because before cars and trains were invented, a journey was something that took time, effort and planning. You had to prepare yourself for it and make sure that you'd packed up everything you needed – including a decent map. It's foolish to travel somewhere new without a good map.

In fact, there's nothing more frustrating than realising you've been taking the exact same route to a well-known destination for years, only to discover that there was a shortcut that you could have taken all along. Which is one of the reasons we all need books like this one.

If you are new to sales and business development – and they seem like strange, uncharted, foreign lands – then you'll want to put your trust in an experienced guide as you travel through. And for those of you who see yourselves as old sales war horses, if you've been round the block a few times, I'd share this:

No one knows where the shortcut is until they're shown it.

What if that block you know so well is actually the long way round?

It has been my experience that people exchange their money for things that they *trust* and see *value* in. I believe that in *Converted*, Matt Sykes has crafted a book that will deliver incredible value to anyone who needs to grow their business and improve a number of related skill sets.

So, back to my original question – what are you hoping for?

I reckon, if you're looking to grow your business – then this book is a good choice.

If you'd like to have more productive meetings with prospects and clients – then this book would be a good choice.

And if you would like to know how to create a structured, well thought-out road map to business-to-business sales success – then this book is definitely a good choice.

But I'd like to add a caveat: your implementation of these ideas will be crucial to your success. You have got to absorb the knowledge in these pages and then put it to work. I've found that success usually takes a decent map, the right amount of preparation and a willingness to take the journey.

I hope you realise whatever it is that you are hoping to achieve. I know that you are in safe hands with Matt Sykes. Here's to your success.

Chris Murray, author of *The Extremely Successful Salesman's Club* and *Selling with EASE*
May 2020

Introduction

What were you doing when you made your very first sale – do you remember?

How about your next one?

Where will your next sale come from?

When will your next meaningful sales conversation happen and what will you do to make certain you close the sale?

How do you respond when a prospect says 'I'd like to think it over, call me in a couple of weeks'? How about when you send a quotation and the customer disappears, avoiding returning your calls? How do you reply when a potential customer says, 'it's too expensive' and how do you avoid reducing your price but still keep the sale alive?

If you're unsure about how to respond to any of these questions, read on. The answers lie in the pages that follow, uncovered over twenty years spent in the business-to-business (B2B) sales industry. Knowing the answers to these questions is what separates those who know how to convert more leads into sales and those who don't.

Have you noticed that some sales professionals seem able to build rapport effortlessly? It's the same people who seem able to get commitment from buyers from the very start and are able to keep control of the sale right to the end. They rarely encounter objections. And as for those elaborate 1980s closing techniques that the old-fashioned sales gurus still bang on about today – irrelevant. The best salespeople seem to let their customers close the sale themselves.

By the end of this book, you'll know how they achieve this and just like them, you'll have a method for converting more opportunities into orders. I'm going to unpack and show you the sales process from start to finish. I'll give you exercises, tips and strategies to help you avoid wasting time with people who'll never buy what you sell and show you how to reduce the time it takes to close a sale with those who will. This book will give you everything you need to convert more of your leads into cash.

Selling is possibly the oldest profession known to man, yet probably the least understood. I've witnessed many new hires be given a phone, a laptop and a territory on day one who are told, 'Well done, you're now a salesperson.' Is it any wonder so many struggle to achieve, and leave the profession so quickly?

If you think selling should be easier than it is, and if you're looking for a proven sales methodology based on logic and results, then this book offers you just that.

I ask the 'What were you doing when you made your very first sale?' question a lot. It's the first question I serve up to the guests who join me on my podcast and it's my opening line to the audience when I speak on stage. While the responses are sometimes random, what their feedback confirms each and every time is that everyone has a clear interest in sales. It's my belief that everyone is in sales. You and I are getting paid for selling goods and services, but teachers are selling education to their students. The pupils in their classes are persuading their parents that they don't need to do their homework – they are selling the idea to them. Their parents are selling themselves to their employer to secure a promotion or a pay rise. The CEO is selling the vision, mission and values of that business to their employees, and the employees' ability to sell those concepts to their customers will have a significant impact on the success or failure of that organisation.

When you look at it this way, we are all selling something.

In my line of work, you meet a lot of outstanding sales trainers, sales directors and salespeople. Irrespective of whether they've stumbled backwards into a sales role in their mid-forties or found sales at the age of six by selling lemonade to thirsty drivers, I've yet to meet a 'born salesperson'. No one enters the world knowing how to sell. Selling is a science that is brought to life with just the right amount of art – it's nurture not nature.

Selling, or rather, being good at helping people buy what you sell, is a learnable skill just like any other. This book is going to teach you how to convert a lead into a sale.

Allow me to introduce myself. I'm a sales professional, business owner and author. I'm an eternal optimist and I'm 100% committed to challenging the negative way the sales industry is often viewed. Contrary to popular opinion, I believe that selling should be seen as a force for good.

It was my optimism that drove me to quit the comfort and safety of a steady nine to five job in favour of living a life on my terms: being my own boss, earning a commission-only salary and living or dying by my results – no-one else's. I entered the professional world of selling in 1998 as a sales representative and made it to European Sales Director before quitting to work for myself in 2014.

As I transition into my third decade in the B2B sales industry, my objective for this, my second book, is to help you do what I do, which is to adopt a proven process that allows you to convert more leads into sales. Whether you're on the payroll in a corporate sales job or you're a self-employed entrepreneur, there are two fundamental things you need to be able to sell.

First, you need to get your product or service in front of plenty of the right people and help them see that what you offer is good for them. Second, you need to do it in a systematic and logical way so that the vast majority of those conversations convert into cash. This book has been written to provide you with everything you need to achieve those two fundamental goals.

The online world, as wonderful as it is, has conned us all into thinking that 'sales has changed' and that 'people buy differently now'. While there is some truth that buyer behaviour has been influenced by the advent of the internet, the reality is that some things have not changed as much as we might think. There is a well-known saying, 'People do business with people they know, like and trust.' This still holds true, in my experience.

Almost every business will spend a small fortune on elaborate websites, lead generation magnets and

Search Engine Optimisation software to create a steady flow of leads, yet few invest the same level of effort and resource in making sure those leads convert into payback. Ask yourself: how much money have you spent on tools to improve marketing, compared to skills that create sales?

Business life became a whole lot easier for me when I figured out that sales is much like telling a story. It's a sequence of interlinked steps that, one after the other, play out a story until the ending reveals itself. In the chapters that follow, I'm going to share what those interlinked steps are. Once you've completed them, you'll always follow and take your prospect along with you on the same logical journey.

As with all personal development, you hold the key to this book, not me. The gift that you have for self-improvement should be celebrated. In my opinion, founded on years spent training sales professionals, only the highest performing people aspire to learn new things.

The rewards that come with finding more sales are many. For some, that could mean more choice – such as the gift to choose how and where to earn your living and to select whom you want to sell to. For others, the reward may be financial. The profession of selling can offer earnings where the sky is the limit, and while the ground might be a tad too close right now for some readers of this book, it's only a matter of time before your newfound understanding of how to convert more sales will start to raise you higher, towards achieving your true earning potential.

I hope you enjoy reading *Converted* as much as I enjoyed writing it and I wish you the same sales success you wish for yourself and are capable of achieving.

1 Resilience

Most people who know anything about selling will agree that the very first sale you have to make is with yourself. At the end of this chapter, you'll have a sound understanding of how to do that, the importance of mindset and attitude – both yours and your customers' – and an awareness of how to leverage it in your sales role.

This first chapter is a bit of a bonus. To some extent, it sits outside of the sales process I'm going to share with you in the chapters that follow. But so valuable is it, in its ability to help you make the most out of the rest of the book, it has to go first. It's priceless.

The buyer's psychology

Whether we like it or not, like all relationships, selling is a 'contact sport', in that it can't take place without interaction with others. We need two people to make a sale happen. On occasion, personalities clash, egos collide and things can get uncomfortable. But in my experience, most salespeople I meet avoid conflict. After all, it's not rocket science. Tell the buyer what they want to hear, and they'll buy – right?

Wrong!

In fact, the exact opposite is true. The more you question a buyer's motive, the greater the chance that you'll convert that prospect into a sale. It sounds counterintuitive but knowing how to positively challenge a potential customer and – respectfully – make life uncomfortable for them, is the foundation for converting more leads into sales.

By the end of this chapter on emotional resilience, you'll understand the role your mindset plays in your sales results. You can choose to be a people-pleaser, one who avoids conflict and seeks out approval, or you can develop the attitude of a true sales professional, one who plants their feet and confidently takes a prospect to the edge of their comfort zone. Sales is not about being liked, it's about being trusted and that comes from being brutally honest with the prospect.

That last point carries a certain amount of irony. Buyers lie to salespeople. It's part of the buyer's psychology, something that's evolved over many, many years as a direct result of the way salespeople have interacted with buyers over time. If we're going to become resilient in our pursuit of making sales, we first need to understand what's going on inside the buyer's head.

Let's look at four overarching psychology traits that prospects adopt.

First, right from the start, they have deep reluctance to believe anything that salespeople say – a bit of a deal-breaker, wouldn't you agree? There are genuine reasons why buyers struggle to accept the words of salespeople. For years, they've been conditioned to believe that a salesperson's job is to aggressively sell them something they don't want or need, possibly using deceitful tactics. Hollywood has propagated the stereotype with films like *The Wolf of Wall Street* and sadly, society continues to hold on to the clichéd image of salespeople as sharp-talking, shiny suit-wearing con artists. Is it any wonder that a buyer would be reluctant to be open and honest with someone like that?

"Talk to the hand cos the face aint listening."

Second, buyers are incredibly sceptical of anything that salespeople show them – like a company brochure, or testimonials on a website. In an online world of 'clickbait' marketing copy and narcissistic LinkedIn posts promoting how great businesses are and how awesome their product is, this is easy to understand. The golden rule in selling is that people buy for their reasons, not yours, and promoting anything other than value for the customer is pointless, as buyers may not find other reasons to buy persuasive or credible.

Third, identifying who a buyer will believe and trust can be unpredictable in surprising ways. To give an example, I could tell my wife about the benefits and virtues of Vinyasa Flow Yoga and she may brand it 'fake news'. Yet, if that same topic pops up on her Facebook feed from someone she's never met, it may become newsworthy for her. There can be complex social factors behind which people exert influence over a buyer, and why.

Knowing these three traits should give you a head start to positively impact your sales strategy and also your confidence, a key component of emotional resilience. You now know that certain buyers may think about you in certain ways, especially at the start of the sales conversation. Unless we work with that dynamic, we'll restrict our ability to progress the sale. Which brings us to the last trait to be aware of.

Buyer psychology trait number four (no surprise here, folks), is that a buyer will always believe what they say *themselves*. So, press pause on your elevator pitch and put away your brochures until after I've shown you how to get a prospect to tell themselves (and you) that they want to buy what you're selling. Until then, let's focus on building your mental toughness so that you're ready for when that day comes.

Think and grow rich

In my first book, *Sales Glue*, I shared the link between how salespeople think and how that impacts their results, both positively and negatively. I described how we're programmed and wired to think first and act second – even 'fight or flight' behaviour is driven by a split-second thought. But that thinking, or cognitive architecture that you've built for yourself, can be redesigned and the best part is you don't need to have a PhD in Performance Psychology to do it.

If you're willing to accept that we don't 'just do things' unthinkingly (other than the obvious bodily functions like breathing) then you already have the basic fundamentals required to master your sales resilience.

If we take the key principle that:

thoughts + activity = results

we can see that we'll actually improve our results if we're willing to adjust our behaviour and the thoughts that drive it.

Let's look at some examples. Take frustration for instance. No one likes feeling frustrated. Imagine you are sitting in a tiresome sales meeting hosted by a sales manager. The meeting involves a line by line interrogation of the CRM, a humiliating analysis of the aged debtors list and sporadic interruptions as the presenter pauses to reach for their phone every time it goes 'ping'!

Whenever we feel that frustration, we have a number of ways to deal with it. First, we could do nothing at all. Sit there in a self-induced coma and ride it out. Doing nothing is a reasonable option to take. But it is unlikely to change the misery you find yourself in.

Second, we could do the opposite. We could do something (though please resist the temptation to chin your boss, as your course of action needs to serve you well in the long term!). A more constructive act could be to respectfully ask your boss for the opportunity to chair the next sales meeting, allowing you to tactfully share your suggestions of what a great sales meeting could look like.

If taking action doesn't appeal to you, you can still take matters into your own hands and arguably get a better result with the final option. You could recognise that if you can't control, or you opt not to change the situation, you *can* control what you think about it. If you change the way you think about the predicament you find yourself in, the predicament will change – this is called a reframe.

You may think it's your boss and their appalling meeting that's responsible for your frustration, but it's not. You've chosen to think negatively and it's your thoughts that have created that feeling of frustration. It's on you to take some responsibility, deploy a dose of emotional resilience and take back control of your thoughts and feelings. Here's how.

Replace that feeling of frustration (an emotional state that's clearly not serving you well) and substitute it with a feeling of curiosity. Ask yourself how you would host the meeting if you were in charge? How would you do things differently? What ideas could you come up with to bring engagement, inspiration and influence to a room that is clearly in need of all three?

Or, instead of curiosity, try sympathy. Maybe they aren't great at sales management, but research shows that 43% of sales managers don't receive effective training prior to taking up their role. Surely you can have sympathy for someone who was plucked from sales stardom by senior management and thrust into managing a team of different personalities without learning how to.

If curiosity or sympathy don't do it for you, try acceptance. After all, it's not you up the front of the room with your jazz hands out making a total arse of yourself.

The point is this: whatever you're doing, whatever you're experiencing, it's you who's in control of your emotions, based on how you think about what's in front of you and you get to choose how you feel. And that is one massive, gold-plated piece of sales weaponry to have at your disposal as we progress through this book.

From this moment forward, no buyer can ever make you feel the misery that comes with sales rejection ever again. Feeling rejected is an emotion and it comes from your thoughts, not their words. Don't want to feel rejected? Either do something to avoid it happening or accept that it sometimes will – even for the best in the business – and try to think differently about it.

Sometimes, the whole personal development movement gets a bad rap. Listen, I struggle with those fluffy motivational quotes on Instagram as much as the next guy. But if there is one thing I train my clients' sales teams to focus on more than anything else, it's mindset. There is literally nothing more inspiring or dynamic than a trained sales professional with a positive attitude. Remember the formula – the actions you take only go half way to creating the results that you want. When you understand the power of the mind in this equation, you really can think and grow rich.

Get off the couch!

Have you ever wondered why two salespeople in the same sales team, with the same product, same boss, similar territories, same weekly working hours, can speak, behave and perform completely differently?

Ever noticed that some salespeople use blame a lot when they talk about what a customer has said or hasn't done? They may also find justifications for why customers object, why deals haven't closed and why they could be so much better at this selling game if only other people would do their job properly? It's as if these people have washed their hands of determining their own destiny.

Have you pondered the notion that you could well be the only salesperson in your company who's decided to further their personal development by reading this book? After all, you didn't have to read this – you could be lying on your couch watching *Game of Thrones*. But the difference between you and the couch version of you is that, by reading this, you have taken responsibility.

In my experience, many salespeople I meet know what it means to take responsibility, yet many struggle to actually take it. They are left sitting on the couch. These are the salespeople who don't get stuff done. What's more, they don't see that it's their own inactivity – not the buyer's – which is affecting their results. You'll know a couch person by the following hallmarks:

- They haven't got enough leads because they don't prospect enough.

- They waste time giving away free advice because they don't know how to qualify their prospects.

- They have a lifetime membership to a buyer's voicemail because they don't control the sale.

But you're different. You read books, listen to podcasts, invest in your personal development. Sure, you need some help – we all do – but the key point is, you're taking responsibility for what happens next and that's what makes you different. That's what will make you successful.

Unleash your latent potential

In 2013, I was a sales director in a corporate job. There was stress, pressure, 150 emails a day and the constant challenge of protecting my team from the 'trigger-happy' senior management, but it was a steady job and one that paid me good money every month, guaranteed. From the outside looking in, I'd made it.

The reality on the inside was somewhat different. I was locked behind my laptop, I rarely got out to see my customers and when I did, it reminded me of the job I was born to do rather than the one I found myself in. I was desperately unhappy.

So, I took responsibility and left the safety and comfort of corporate employment and acted out my very own exit scene from *Jerry McGuire*. I walked away from a six-figure package and headed into a world of the unknown, challenging myself with a brave new world of self-employment, a commission-only salary and a totally new career.

Reckless? Possibly. Risky? Definitely. Liberating? Absolutely!

There's something about taking responsibility for your own destiny that brings out the best in people. Since leaving the comfort of the nine to five, I've built a training business, written two books, spoken on stages in front of hundreds of people and established a podcast, and all of this happened because I took responsibility. If I hadn't, that latent potential would still be there. Hidden, dormant, wasted.

It's my belief that we all have latent potential. Not everyone wants to unleash it, but plenty could. That includes you.

Design your future

Let's say you do decide to take more responsibility for converting more leads into sales. You take the advice, strategies and tips from this book and apply them, daily. Fast-forward six months. What would need to have happened to allow you to say, 'Thank goodness I took responsibility and took action back then!'?

Here's a quick exercise to help you answer that. Over the next five minutes, why not design your future? Consider the following questions and write down exactly what you want to happen six months from now:

- What do your sales results look like?

- What's happening in your career?

- How many new customers will you have?
- What impact is your sales success having on your personal life?

With this vision in mind, let's think about the small changes you can make – today – to help you get there. Here are just a handful of the many ways you can take responsibility and increase accountability to make your design a reality.

Organise your to-do list

Please tell me you have a to-do list, otherwise this first tip is pointless! Sort your tasks into three categories:

1. Admin tasks that need to be done, but cost you time (Desk job).

2. High-value, high-return actions that lead to a sale, like prospecting (Day job).

3. Strategic activities that might lead to sales in the future, like marketing (Dream job).

Aim to spend at least 70% of your day doing the 'Day job' tasks but be sure to leave some time, every day, for the 'Dream job' activities – these are the ones your future self will thank you for.

Make prospecting a daily activity. This is important even when things are going well and the pipeline is healthy, so that your tonality and body language can continue to come from a position of confidence rather than desperation. We'll talk more about prospecting in chapter two.

Be upfront with buyers

Take control and lead the customer along their buying process (your sales process) – it will deliver a more meaningful outcome for you both. Share and justify your key objectives in advance and insist on a mutual agreement to take action after you've finished. In short, explain at the start of your conversation what their options will be at the end. Provided your solution demonstrates a perceived value for them – and it better had – they will understand this approach and be accepting of being shown the direction towards achieving their payback.

We'll discover in chapter three the importance of starting every scheduled call or meeting with a verbal agenda. There is no greater crime in the sales world than leaving a meeting without a call to action.

Engage with your customer base

Spend more time with your existing clients – especially the 'silent majority', the ones whom we naively believe will be customers forever. The ones who never complain or ask for help. If there's one thing worse than not growing sales organically, it's not being able to retain existing clients.

It's your responsibility to not allow the clients who've already trusted you with their business to leave for reasons that you *can* control. To do this, you must be really close to them. You have to know the conversation that's going on inside their head and to do that, you need to talk to them regularly and get their feedback.

Measure twice, cut once

I can't remember if it was my dad's advice or simply as a result of trial and error, but there's a phrase that immediately comes to mind when I'm in DIY mode. On the rare occasions that my wife actually trusts me to do odd jobs around the house, especially the ones that involve power tools, I always think of the phrase 'Measure twice, cut once'.

That one simple rule has saved me hours in lost time and cost my local hardware store a fortune in lost wood sales. It applies to all walks of life, including sales. By double-checking before taking action, we can confirm that what we're about to do makes sense. It's this logic that I want you to apply to this section of the book. If you want to find out which areas of your sales ability need improving, you need to measure them first.

The following Salescadence Competence Audit is designed specifically for you to consider the statement, select your answer and score yourself. Each of these fifty-five statements relates to the chapters of this book, but before you discover how, go ahead and complete the audit. You can fill it out here or head over to www.salescadence.co.uk/salescadence-competence-audit and complete it online if you prefer. Either way, take the audit!

Circle the number which most fits with your thoughts on the subject and *be honest*! Honesty is critical to you learning from this exercise so don't cheat yourself.

THE SALESCADENCE COMPETENCE AUDIT

Score: 1 – Never 2 – Occasionally 3 – Sometimes 4 – Often 5 – Always	
1. I focus daily on what I want to achieve	1 2 3 4 5
2. I view every outcome of each sales call as positive and useful	1 2 3 4 5
3. I see sales rejection as a way to help me improve	1 2 3 4 5
4. I handle my emotional state well, both in work and at home	1 2 3 4 5
5. I adopt positive beliefs for myself about my ability	1 2 3 4 5
6. I know how many calls I need to make each week to hit quota	1 2 3 4 5
7. I prospect for new business every day	1 2 3 4 5
8. I have products that build trust and engagement with prospects	1 2 3 4 5
9. I know exactly who my ideal customer is	1 2 3 4 5

10.	I spend time building and developing my personal brand	1 2 3 4 5
11.	I engage, like, comment and post on LinkedIn everyday	1 2 3 4 5
12.	I have a well-rehearsed pitch that creates instant engagement	1 2 3 4 5
13.	I focus on disqualifying prospects as soon as possible	1 2 3 4 5
14.	I listen well	1 2 3 4 5
15.	I receive willing co-operation from people	1 2 3 4 5
16.	I write down my key objectives in advance of every sales call	1 2 3 4 5
17.	I create a pre-call plan for every prospect or customer meeting	1 2 3 4 5
18.	I control the sales conversation in every prospect meeting	1 2 3 4 5
19.	I end every meeting with a call to action	1 2 3 4 5
20.	I write a post-call debrief after every sales call	1 2 3 4 5
21.	I resist talking about my product/service until I know it's required	1 2 3 4 5
22.	I have a set of flexible, strategic questions that lead to a close	1 2 3 4 5
23.	I ask for a buyer's commitment before sharing product information	1 2 3 4 5
24.	I always ask the prospect to share their objectives at the start	1 2 3 4 5
25.	I resist talking about price until I know they want to buy	1 2 3 4 5
26.	I establish who the decision-makers are at the start of the call	1 2 3 4 5
27.	I always ask the prospect what their ultimate motive is	1 2 3 4 5

28.	I insist on making sure the prospect has the funds to buy	1 2 3 4 5
29.	I walk the buyer through the steps of the sale in advance	1 2 3 4 5
30.	I establish an early collaborative relationship with buyers	1 2 3 4 5
31.	I take time to fully clarify the prospect's reason for buying	1 2 3 4 5
32.	I always make sure the problem they have is monetarised	1 2 3 4 5
33.	I ask '5 why' questions to uncover the root cause of their pain	1 2 3 4 5
34.	I ask the prospect to calculate their ROI before talking solutions	1 2 3 4 5
35.	I work hard to mitigate the buyer's risk before asking for the sale	1 2 3 4 5
36.	I know why prospects object	1 2 3 4 5
37.	I always ask a prospect to justify their objection	1 2 3 4 5
38.	I view objections as my fault	1 2 3 4 5
39.	I already know the objections a prospect will have	1 2 3 4 5
40.	I know the exact response for every objection I hear	1 2 3 4 5
41.	I only send a quotation if I'm sure it will convert to an order	1 2 3 4 5
42.	I insist on a pre-meeting to discuss an RFP (request for proposal)	1 2 3 4 5
43.	I include risk-reversal clauses in my proposals	1 2 3 4 5
44.	I provide a range of options in every proposal I send	1 2 3 4 5

45.	I send proposals only if a buyer agrees to meet to discuss it	1 2 3 4 5
46.	I have a systematic process for keeping contact with customers	1 2 3 4 5
47.	I actively seek referrals	1 2 3 4 5
48.	I always ask for a case study once the sale is completed	1 2 3 4 5
49.	I send regular valuable information and insights to my customers	1 2 3 4 5
50.	My customers view me as a strategic advisor to their business	1 2 3 4 5
51.	I regularly learn new sales skills	1 2 3 4 5
52.	I know which areas of my sales skills I must improve	1 2 3 4 5
53.	I focus all my time on 'high-value, high-revenue' activity	1 2 3 4 5
54.	My boss would describe me as a high-performer	1 2 3 4 5
55.	I am passionate about the product/service I sell	1 2 3 4 5

Plot your score on the following scale:
55……….110……….165……….220……….275

Congratulations! That one simple exercise has not only stirred up a whole load of evidence to help you find more sales, but it's also put you ahead of the competition. In my experience, few salespeople invest in their personal development, and of the many I've met, trained and mentored over the last twenty years, few have an idea about which areas of their sales behaviour need improving.

Listen, I'm a realist. Of course, there's a variety of reasons why many salespeople don't seek to improve and we'll explore a number of these reasons later in the book. But for now, take solace in the fact you're already one step ahead. And if you want to take another step, turn the page and keep moving forward! But just before you go…

WHAT'S ONE THING YOU COULD DO TODAY?

Put a date in your calendar exactly ninety days from today's date and retake the Competence Audit. Benchmark your score and plot how and where you have improved.

---

2 Reach

It's not rocket science. If you want more sales, you need to identify the right people to talk to and then talk to them in such a way that results in a sale. Selling is a relatively simple process that people tend to over-complicate. It doesn't have to be like that. As you'll learn in this book, a great sales process is a series of steps travelled in sequence and with purpose.

When you get to the end of this chapter, you'll know how to reach more of the people who want to buy what you sell. This will allow you to spend quality time developing your strategic approach to finding the right leads and ultimately closing more sales.

Let's get into it.

The Ideal Customer Profile

Are there any customers you wish you didn't have?

For a variety of reasons, agreeing to serve them was the right thing for you to do at the time. You were just starting out and really needed the business, perhaps. Maybe you saw them as an opportunity to get a referral, or they offered you the chance to add another logo to the 'About' page of your website. All valid justifications and, frankly, necessary when you're trying to grow your sales.

I've been there, and I know that business from customers like these is a poisoned chalice. No sooner has the ink dried on their contract, the reality of what you've signed up for starts to become clearer. Compared to what they actually expect from you, their original brief now looks like a work of fiction. These customers usually expect much more than they're willing to pay for and they rarely pay on time. Very frustrating.

Hanging around with the wrong type of customers *is* frustrating. It's costly and it's potentially damaging for your business. There are more than enough of the wrong type of customers out there and each of them will make life difficult for you – if you allow them to.

What we'll discover in this chapter is the importance of seeking out and engaging with only the right customer for your business. The ones who truly want to work with you. The ones who not only bring out the best in you but also want *you* to succeed. 'Who are these people you speak of, Matt?', I hear you cry…

Ladies and gentlemen, I give you 'The Ideal Customer Profile' or, as it's more commonly known, the ICP. It's one of the primary components of sales success.

Before you can reach out to your ICP, you must first find out who they are, what they look like and what gets them interested in having conversations with people like you. Spending quality time identifying your ICP will not only lead you to have more sales conversations, but also more meaningful ones with a higher likelihood of success.

The first question to ask yourself is, where are they located? Sounds obvious, I know, but until you know where they are, how can you reach them? Their location, or 'geographic profile', is really important if, for example, you're selling a service and you'll be meeting with them regularly to deliver that service. Your cost of sales (and home life) might suffer if your ICP is located on the other side of the country. You may, on the other hand, be willing to provide an online service if your ICP's location calls for it.

The next thing to consider is your ICP's 'demographic profile' – whether they fall within a certain age group, have a specific level of education and type of occupation. If your ICP is over fifty, you might be wasting your time trying to engage with them on TikTok. If their role requires a high level of education or technical knowledge – a surgeon, solicitor or CTO, for example – you can expect that they'll want to converse at that level with you.

Consider also their income, their company's financial viability and growth potential. With such a rapid move towards artificial intelligence, there's a stark reality that certain jobs will be at risk of automation in the future, so the potential for a decline in growth must also be a consideration. Be certain that you're not setting up your business to attract customers who might not be around in the not too distant future.

It's also helpful to understand as much as possible about their 'personality profile' so that we can engage with them on their terms. Being able to communicate with them in a way that captures their interest is key. There is an abundance of personality profiles available to help you, like DISC®[1] or MBTI®[2], as well as software like Crystal Knows[3], which can analyse someone's LinkedIn profile and provide you with insights into the personality who wrote it and advice on how to engage with them.

Gathering data for these three important profiles will clarify who is the ideal customer to fit your needs.

---

1   www.discprofile.com/what-is-disc/overview/
2   www.myersbriggs.org/my-mbti-personality-type/mbti-basics/home.htm?bhcp=1
3   www.crystalknows.com/

Chances are, you will already have a customer in your portfolio who fits that description and if that is the case, you simply need to find more like them.

Problems and solutions

As we discussed in the first chapter, people buy for their reasons, not ours. If we get a call from the local car dealership saying, 'Great news, we've got a car here for you today, head over and buy it now!', we don't buy the car because they want us to. Whenever we buy anything, it's because we have a reason to buy it. We'll go to the car dealer when we're ready to buy a new car, simple as that.

Another key principle to remember is that people only ever buy two things: a solution to a problem or an improvement to something that already exists. If there's no problem, no pain, then there's no need for a solution – and a solution is the thing that leads to a sale. Run out of dishwasher tablets? Head to the supermarket and get some more. Feeling peckish? Give the local Chinese a call and satisfy your craving. Feel like you're not good enough at sales? Buy a book and learn some new ways to up your sales game.

Understanding the reasons people buy allows us to build out our ICP. Ask yourself, what are the big problems your ICP has when they come to you for help? List them. There's probably three really big ones – absolute showstoppers – and if you know what these are, you can engage your ICP by talking about them. Think of it like poking them with a stick – just hard enough to get their attention.

Now that you've grabbed them, and have perhaps riled them by talking about their problems, you need to know how to calm them down. This the easy part. It's not time to explain how your product or service offers them a solution yet, we'll cover when to do this later in the book. For now, simply jot down the 'customer benefits' of your product or service next to each of the ICP problems you identified and prepare for when that conversation comes.

Most sales people are expert at 'vomiting' their features and benefits all over anyone who remotely looks like a prospect and while we'll learn later why this is absurd, at this stage knowing what your product or service does allows you to assign these 'customer benefits' next to each of the ICP problems.

Over the next fifteen minutes, why not get really clear on who your ICP is? Use the five points below as a guide and build up a profile of exactly what your ICP looks like:

1. **Geographic profile** – where they're located (city, state, country or continent)

2. **Demographic profile** – their age, education level, profession, economic status

3. **Personality profile** – what they're like as a person
   and what they like to do

4. **Their problems** – what's stopping them from
   achieving their goals

5. **Your solutions** – how your product or service
   solves their problems

A final thought before we move on: how many of your
existing customers fit your ICP and how many of the
prospects in your CRM and pipeline fit it? Maybe it's
time to have a clean-up and remove those who clearly
don't fit. And let's move our attention to finding more
of the ones who do as we move into the next section.

Prospecting

I don't know a single sales professional who enjoys
prospecting. Nuts when you think about it – we're
a sociable bunch who love to meet people and start
conversation, but there's something about outbound
lead generation that turns the stomach and limits the
appetite for doing it.

Yet prospecting – the process of creating leads that
become prospects – is the oxygen for every business.
Without it, you won't have one. I know this simple
truth only too well. When I left the comfort of corporate employment and started my business, the one
thing I'd omitted from my comprehensive, five-year

business plan was finding sales. I'd massively under-estimated the importance of prospecting.

Within a week of self-employment, I learned that a business without leads isn't a business at all. It's a hobby. There's nothing like sitting alone in silence in your office, with bills mounting up and a family to feed, to remind you just how underrated an actual sale is and how important the act of finding them is.

In this section, we're going to build on the work you've done with finding your ICP and look at where your leads are going to come from.

The most obvious place to start is with your existing customers. They've already decided that you're some-one who can be trusted, so before we look at trying to win business from ICPs we don't yet know, let's focus our energy on those we do.

We'll cover customer retention later on in the book, but suffice to say, you should have a strategy in place which allows you to keep in regular contact with all your existing customers. They will provide you with the best opportunity for more business – call them and start a conversation and you'll often find that they're keen to work with you again.

Next, consider your customer's customer. They won't be too dissimilar and will probably have sim-ilar needs, wants and desires. Chances are, you can be introduced to them via a referral – again, there's more on how to do this later in the book. Consider, too, your customer's suppliers. There's real potential here, given that most suppliers will not want to disappoint a customer who makes an introduction. Besides, if you don't ask, you won't find out. It's always worth widening your network like this.

Finally, there are the 'almost customers'. These are the leads that didn't convert into a sale last time. You'll have a load of them sitting in your database, CRM or 'Prospects' folder. The fact that they didn't convert back then doesn't mean to say that you can't try again. If you didn't find out at the time why you lost them, pick up the phone and use that as your opening question. If the timing wasn't right then, it might be now.

Once you've exhausted these opportunities which are 'closer to home', it's time to push into the world of outbound lead generation and start making connections from scratch. Not easy to do, but an essential part of daily life for any sales professional who wants to take responsibility of their sales success.

Back in the day, when I first entered the sales industry, the fax machine was today's smartphone or tablet. The internet was in its infancy and was viewed by many with some suspicion. Email had only just been introduced and a website would set you back tens of thousands of pounds. I can't deny that I struggled to see what value each of these things brought to an already effective sales approach.

Fast-forward to today and it's unimaginable to think what life would be like without websites, iPhones or Google. Factor in the dominance of social media in our personal and business lives, which gives each of us the ability to garner knowledge and self-promote, and it's fair to say that it's never been easier to get in front of prospects.

By blending some of the various communication methods available to you today in a consistent and logical way, you'll give yourself the best possible chance of your prospecting paying off. Let's look at a few.

Post

Often criticised as an old-fashioned method of communication following the advent of email, sending 'lumpy mail' to prospects is now back in vogue and considered innovative. For sure, you need to have a compelling message, but as a way to create early engagement, it's a belter. It takes time and effort to reach customers this way, but if you do this where your competitors won't, you'll stand out. I've sent postcards to warm up cold calls for years because unlike email, I know they'll get read.

Phone

Still the most effective way to get a direct conversation going, although getting someone to take your calls can be difficult. Cold-calling hardly ever works, but warm-calling can. Warm-calling is the ability to increase the chances of creating a 'warm reception' when you reach your prospect and create the best possible chance of starting a conversation. For example, if you've sent a postcard, you might lead with 'What did you think of the postcard?'.

Even so, high double-digit percentage success rates are limited. It is therefore essential to have a well-planned calling strategy to increase the chance of getting a ring-back, and the discipline to follow up when they don't. For me, the phone is my number one recommended prospecting tool.

Email

As a tool for providing information for the recipient, email is hard to beat, but success is limited to and predicated on the recipient opening and reading it. Technology provides the opportunity to insert links and videos to take the reader to the next step of the prospecting journey, but the big challenge with email is overload – your mail is joining a queue of many others in their inbox.

Networking

Of course, building a network is essential when you're finding sales and attending organised events can be a good way to prospect, but it comes with word of caution from me. In my experience, most people who attend events do so as a way to find business, but they don't do it strategically. They wing it. It pays to go in with a plan here, too. Another drawback can come from the event organisers themselves. Sometimes it feels like they're hanging the sword of Damocles over you, waiting to decapitate anyone who tries to sell. Clearly, anyone who actively tries to sell at a networking event has missed the point, because the primary objective is simply to find your ICP. Having conversations based on the problems you solve, not the product you sell, will allow people who fit that profile to identify themselves and engage with you. We'll learn how to do this in the next chapter.

Content marketing

Writing copy that gets attention is essential when it comes to prospecting. Headlines are arguably more important than the article itself, but don't underestimate the value of well-written blogs, posts and sales pages as a mechanism for positioning yourself in front of your ICP. The added benefit of the written word is its ability to be used for targeted search (Search Engine Optimisation, or SEO), so using the keywords that your ICP is searching for in your articles really helps them find you.

Social media

Twitter, Instagram, YouTube and Facebook all offer a global stage to communicate with your ICP, but it's LinkedIn that's regarded as the business prospecting platform. There is a clear focus and acceptance that, provided it's done the right way, growing a network and developing your personal brand is the number one objective of being on LinkedIn. On LinkedIn, you not only have the opportunity to grow your connections and followers, but you can build strong relationships that can (and should) be taken offline and into a meaningful, more personal conversation. These platforms, while helpful when prospecting, aren't enough on their own.

Even the best at social selling, like Daniel Disney, founder of 'The Daily Sales' (LinkedIn's most popular page for salespeople, with over 10 million views on the platform every month), credits his success to first creating engagement online and then taking it off-platform and into a face-to-face sales conversation.[4] Success leaves clues, people. When it comes to social selling, remember the importance of holding a real-life conversation, too, and don't be afraid to move things away from the platform on which you first meet.

_____

4   www.linkedin.com/company/the-daily-sales

LinkedIn offers an incredibly powerful tool to search, connect and start relationships, but if you rely on this and nothing else to prospect for new business, you might be disappointed with the lack of return on your investment. To create genuine *reach*, you need a combination of the right tools and a strategy for how to deploy them so that you show up – consistently, in a number of locations, not just one – and get results.

And that leads me to another significant point about how the sales landscape is rapidly changing and why today's high-achievers recognise the value of building a personal brand.

Personal brand

Chances are, you've had more than one sales job. Who knows, you may have many more moves ahead of you, ideally moves that you choose to instigate rather than being forced on you by an employer. I only changed employer twice during my B2B career, but on both occasions, trying to build relationships with new customers in the same industry felt like starting from scratch.

There will always be an element of starting again when a salesperson moves to a new organisation, but the job becomes harder if you have to build a reputation from scratch, too. Back in the day, the 'little black book' of contacts used to come out and you'd spend a few weeks calling around, letting people know you'd moved. Today, that 'little black book' is called LinkedIn.

It still amazes me that salespeople don't adopt this free platform as their personal website and use it to build their personal brand and grow their reputation. Why wouldn't you want to promote yourself on a business site with more than 650 million other businesspeople on it, especially if some of those people are your customers and potential employers? If people really do buy people, as the saying goes, then surely positioning yourself in front of the people who want to buy what you sell makes sense, doesn't it?

"So, what exactly does a 'Sales Ninja' do?"

The world has changed. By *not* embracing the massive opportunity to build your personal brand, you'll not only miss out on possible sales opportunities – you'll be forgotten.

My advice is this: embrace the world of social media, but follow a strategy and be different. You don't have to be the best, just stand out from the rest. Position yourself as the go-to person in your industry by showing up on LinkedIn regularly and delivering engaging, helpful and targeted content for your ICP based on what you know about them from your profiling exercise. Do this consistently and with purpose and eventually, you'll start to see your efforts rewarded with engagement and inbound enquiries that lead to sales.

Maybe you can progress to hosting your own podcast or writing a book. Both of these take effort, but the beauty of super-charging your prospecting this way is that it creates an audience who comes to listen to you, even while you're asleep. Imagine being able to engage and deliver value to your ICP on demand – what impact might that have on your prospecting?

And should you find yourself leaving a job, you'll have the satisfaction of knowing you're taking all your connections and your personal brand along with you.

What does all this mean for the sales process?

We've looked at the value of having mental and emotional resilience and how you can leverage that by aligning it with ways to help you reach more of the people who want to buy what you sell.

In the next chapter, we're going to find out exactly how to engage with your ICP, and start the conversion process of turning meaningful sales conversations into sales.

Turn the page and let's start that conversation. But just before you do…

WHAT'S ONE THING YOU COULD DO TODAY?

Tidy up your LinkedIn profile. Check out Daniel Disney's profile and use that as inspiration for your own. Make sure you have a professional picture of you smiling and use the 'About' section to share copy that engages your Ideal Customer Profile.

3 Rapport

One of the most popular words in the sales vocabulary and maybe the least understood is 'rapport'. It goes without saying that if our objective is to start a conversation with our Ideal Customer Profile, we must find a way of limiting their resistance to talking to us. We'll need to build rapport with them to warm them to us and convert them from an ideal customer to an actual one.

When you get to the end of this chapter, you'll know exactly what rapport is and the part it plays in converting sales. You'll find out how to engage with prospects on their terms, how to make it easier for them to find you and, of course, what to say to them when they do.

But let me start by telling you what rapport *isn't*.

Rapport isn't that thing you do where you meet with a prospect and spend the first thirty minutes trying to curry favour by talking about everything other than the reason why you're in front of them. The days of filling the silence with banal conversation about their golf handicap or where they're going on their next holiday are over.

Rapport isn't cold-calling someone with the intention of telling them what you do.

Rapport isn't about telling people what you do and how you do it when they ask you what you do.

Why?

Because people can smell disingenuous interest a mile off.

Because people won't listen if you make the conversation all about you.

Because people don't care what you do, they care about what you can do *for them*.

That's why.

Rapport is all about joining the discussion already going on inside the prospect's head or, if there isn't one, it's about helping them to create one, because it will be worth their while to do so.

That's what rapport is.

Entering the sales cycle

When you start to engage with your ICP, they'll naturally want to know more about you. While this sounds like great news, the reality is it only takes a limited amount of time before their curiosity wanes. If they take a look and don't find what they were hoping to find – or worse, find nothing at all – it's over. They're gone, possibly forever!

Every post you write, every video you create has to do two things. It has to be specifically targeted at your ICP and contain valuable information for them. Failing to do this is like throwing spaghetti at a wall and seeing what sticks – messy and, if I'm honest, really weird.

Here's where having a range of easy-to-consume content, often described as 'Products for Prospects' (PFP), can help build rapport and start the process of earning their trust. If you can find a way to allow your ICP to look at, sample and consume what you do without feeling under pressure or being asked to risk investing large sums of money, they will. Think 'try before you buy' or 'taking a test-drive' and you won't be far from helping a prospect enter your sales cycle and moving them through it. Each PFP gradually increases their level of interest and trust in you.

Your PFP system should follow this four-step sequence:

1. **ATTENTION** – They need to notice you first. A series of well-crafted blogs or posts on LinkedIn with engaging or disruptive headlines will help. Commit to putting out a campaign or series over a sustained period of time and you will get attention.

2. **ENGAGEMENT** – Next, engage them. Having your own podcast helps. I started mine, 'The Salescadence Podcast',[5] back in 2018 and it's allowed me to share free content to my ICP, as and when they want to consume it. If you don't have your own podcast, consider starting one or start sharing relevant episodes of podcasts you've heard that your ICP will value.

3. **REVENUE** – ultimately, there will come a time when you need to test your ICP's commitment to buy. It might be too early to put your core product or service in front of them, but a similar product representing a lower-risk investment (such as a book you've written) will help them cross the 'free to fee' chasm.

---

5   www.salescadence.co.uk/podcasts

4. **PROFIT** – with their first purchase justified, their risk reversed and their trust in you confirmed, you can now introduce products with a higher investment level. An example for my business would be a one-to-one Zoom call to review their Salescadence Competence Audit results.

Providing your ICP with PFPs is the most logical way to enter them into your sales cycle. Each step they take in it and every product they consume will reinforce your relevance in their world and build enough trust and confidence for them to want to reach out and engage with you.

Empathy

It would be easy to suggest that in today's world of Facebook, Instagram and Twitter, we have never been more connected. The ease with which we can look and see what our friends and connections are doing and the frequency with which we do it suggest that we've developed a habit for 'checking in'. But are we really connecting with these people or just observing them?

How often have you seen something on social media, and immediately thought, 'What are they doing? Why did they post that? I don't understand why they did that.'?

First published in 1989, *The 7 Habits of Highly Effective People*, by author Stephen Covey, is one of the most highly acclaimed self-help business books of its time, with over 25 million copies sold.[6] The book focuses on aligning one's character and values to life principles. Getting what you want in life requires you to not just do the things that get you there, but to want to get there in the first place.

All seven of Covey's habits have a place in the world of selling, but there is only one habit that is specifically aligned to building rapport. Habit number five is 'seek first to understand, then to be understood' and it teaches us the importance of connection, of allowing the other person to go first, so you can hear and listen to them.

Empathy is about getting interested in the things that interest the people you're interested in. It's a skill like every other sales skill and it's a critical component to being able to convert more sales. Without it, we fail to secure the many benefits on offer. So, what *is* on offer to us if we place empathy at the heart of our sales process?

The first benefit is getting back time. If you've ever been to one of those 'post-mortem' sales meetings to establish why a customer has decided to move to your competition, you'll recall it was pandemonium,

---

6   S Covey, *The 7 Habits of Highly Effective People* (Simon & Schuster, 2004 reprinted edition)

with everyone playing the blame game and throwing one another under the bus. Total chaos! But imagine if everyone in that meeting was able to voice their opinion in turn, making their point and then being quiet until everyone else had done likewise. That one simple act of allowing people to be heard would have knocked hours off most of the sales meetings I've ever attended.

Just so we're clear, this is not about agreeing with people's opinions, it's about agreeing that they have one and that it must be heard. Try bringing that skill into your prospect meetings and see what happens as a consequence. Seek first to understand them before being understood yourself and I guarantee you'll spend your time more efficiently as a result.

The next benefit is also time-related, but it's about how we use it. When we take the time to hear what our prospect has to say, they began to build trust in us, creating the confidence that allows them to share more information with us. Sometimes, this information is crucial to the reason why they need our help and knowing this allows us to fully diagnose the problem and prescribe the right solution.

The benefits of empathy increase when you consider that correct solutions lead to happy customers and happy customers provide repeat business, case studies and referrals, and each of these are components of the sales process that increase the chance of greater sales success. It's not difficult to see that being more empathetic in our approach with prospects, is certainly worth doing. The question is, how do we *do* empathy?

Here are five empathy behaviours. Master these and you'll unlock the benefits:

1. **Be open-minded.** Don't be one of those know-it-all salespeople! Instead, be willing to put aside any preconceived ideas about whether you think you can help a prospect until after you've heard what they have to say.

2. **Be curious.** Stop thinking about what cool thing you're going to say next and start being genuinely interested in what your prospect has to say. Try and find out as much as you can about why they need your help.

3. **Ask meaningful questions.** People buy for *their* reasons, not ours, and the only way of finding out what their reasons are is to ask them. Challenge yourself to ask questions that get to the heart of their reasons.

4. **Listen to understand.** Like crossing a road, poor listeners wait for a gap in the conversation to jump into. Repeat back elements of what your prospect has said and you'll demonstrate that

you've been listening. Hearing yourself respond this way also stimulates your brain to focus on your next response.

5. **Don't interrupt.** Avoid completing a prospect's sentence for them – it's really annoying! Instead, give people the time and space to say what's on their mind and they'll usually keep talking. Use the power of a pause to your advantage: they'll fill the vacant space if you create it.

Pitching

Ever found yourself in an elevator talking to a complete stranger? How about making conversation based on what you sell, with the sole aim of getting the other person excited about how they can buy it? No? Me neither.

I've been in hundreds of elevators over the last twenty years and not one opportunity like that has ever presented itself to me. I'm either hanging around in the wrong high-rise buildings or the 'elevator pitch' is a work of fiction, some magical idea created for movies to depict the 'cut and thrust' of the stereotypical salesperson.

"This is my elevator pitch and trust me, you'll love it!"

Yet pitching is a key component of the prospecting strategy and something that, when done well, can open and close a sale. When you have a well-crafted and well-rehearsed pitch that you can deliver 'on demand', doing so without sounding scripted, allowing your words to flow naturally, engaging the listener, tapping into their curiosity, then you open up opportunities for yourself.

Despite my earlier sarcasm, the elevator pitch actually did happen and its history dates back to the nineteenth century when Elisha Otis, founder of the Otis Elevator Company, was looking for a way to resolve the fears that the public had of riding in them. He invented a safety system that would stop elevators from free-falling and put on a public demonstration in New York City.

His practical test worked and the crowd erupted with applause. They were able to see first-hand that using an elevator was not only safe, but would also save them time. Shortly after his pitch, Otis founded his elevator business, one that continues to serve billions of people every year with products located in thousands of buildings around the world.

This story gives obvious insights into what makes a great pitch. Clearly, we need a product, and one that serves a specific market. We also need an Ideal Customer Profile to pitch to. There needs to be some benefit for them, a successful outcome. In the case of Otis, his invention made life easier for those wishing to work in tall buildings. But dig a little deeper and we'll see that for early engagement to happen, a pitch needs to focus on solving a problem, too.

Not every pitch is the same, of course. On occasion, we need to adjust a pitch to the specific objective. There are different pitches designed for different scenarios. For example, when meeting a prospect for the first time, you need to not only create instant engagement, but also establish if they might fit your ICP.

If you're pitching to someone you already have an existing relationship with, it's less about engagement and more about qualification – are they in a position to want what you sell and if so, do they want it now or in the future?

There are three unique pitches and each one serves a purpose. They are the 'social pitch', the 'scheduled pitch' and the 'sales pitch'. We'll cover the latter two later in the book, so for now, let's focus on the one designed to start a sales conversation.

The social pitch

Included in your prospecting strategy should be time allocated to spend at networking events, business seminars and trade shows. The upside of these gatherings is, of course, people and usually people who are willing to engage with you. After all, they're also there themselves to find prospects.

But there are two big problems with these events. First, most people you meet for the first time at functions like these are unlikely to fit your ICP, so unless you have a method of establishing that pretty quickly, you could waste valuable time talking to the wrong people.

Second, you wouldn't start a conversation in a pub with a stranger and say, 'Hi, Ed, good to meet you. Now listen, let me tell you all about me and how great I am.' I'm not joking either, you too have probably been on the receiving end of people who do that at networking events, namely vomiting their features and benefits all over you!

A really good social pitch solves those two problems. It's typically no more than thirty seconds in duration and has the primary objective of placing the listener at the heart of the conversation. It also does it in such a way that it disqualifies anyone who doesn't fit your ICP.

Most salespeople try to 'qualify in' rather than 'disqualify out' because they think 'everyone's a customer'. This deluded thinking drives them to go for a 'Yes' rather than a 'No', and so begins a long and painful relationship that usually results in endless 'free consulting' for the salesperson, helping someone who'll never buy from them. To avoid this, your social pitch has to align itself with the conversation going on inside the listener's head.

Let me explain the social pitch process:

1. **Permission.** When someone asks you what you do, ask their permission before you respond. This immediately distinguishes you from everyone else who doesn't do this; it acts as a 'pattern-interrupt' and gets their attention for what's about to follow. It's also good old-fashioned common courtesy, something that's a rare and valuable commodity these days. Try asking, 'Would it be OK with you if I give you a couple of examples of the people I serve and why they come to me for help?'

2. **Profile.** To start the disqualification process, you need to let the listener know who you work with, because you now have certain specific people you're looking for – your ICP. Something like, 'I work with CEOs and sales directors located in South-East England, who have overall responsibility for the success of a sales team of up to fifty salespeople.'

3. **Problem.** Psychologically, we're blessed with something called a negativity bias. It's the thing responsible for that Monday-morning feeling! But it's really helpful for creating engagement as it kicks in our pain response, hence why you should always pitch the problem *before* a solution if you want to get their attention. An example: 'Typically, they come to me to solve two big problems. First, they win business, but they're in a competitive market and so it's business won on price, with paper-thin margins. Second, buyers dictate the pace of the sale and string their team along, wasting hours trying to follow up rather than moving the sale forward.'

4. **Progress.** The key to a successful social pitch is making sure something happens at the end. Not doing this is like leaving a meeting without agreeing next steps, actions and due dates – pointless. A direct question will get resisted, because everyone finds it hard to admit they need help, even if they do. Talking in 'third-party' terms protects them but allows you to still ask

the question. Try this: 'I see these problems all the time in the market. [Describe the problems.] So, just out of curiosity, does anyone in your network come to mind now that I've said that?'

Delivering a social pitch this way gives you a better chance of entering the conversation going on inside the other person's head. It draws them into the discussion and triggers their natural 'fight or flight' survival instincts. If your pitch leaves them thinking, 'Do I have these problems? Have I had them in the past? Might I have them again? Do I know anyone else who does?', you've cracked it!

What does all this mean for the sales process?

We've established in this chapter that people need time to build trust in both us and our product before they'll buy. In some cases, a prospect will need between eight and twelve 'touches' (encounters with your product or organisation) and consume hours of content before they feel ready to reach out and start a meaningful sales conversation.

Making that content available and easy to find is crucial, so use your website copy, LinkedIn and YouTube and build a range of PFPs to engage them and build their trust in you.

Master the skill of empathy. Learn and deploy the behaviours which allow you to understand your customer before being understood yourself.

Create, practise and perfect your social pitch. Be comfortable with the fact that most people you meet for the first time in a social environment may not want what you sell, so approach these conversations with a mindset of protecting yourself from those you can't serve. Seek to 'disqualify out' first, with a view to 'qualifying in' second.

OK, we're really starting to build momentum. Now that we've covered prospecting and starting conversations, let's move on to see how we can maximise these interactions and convert them into genuine sales opportunities. But first...

WHAT'S ONE THING YOU COULD DO TODAY?

Once you've created your social pitch, video yourself delivering it and then watch it back. If it looks natural and believable to you, chances are, it will for your prospect. Practise it daily. Pitch yourself by leaving a voicemail – do this until you've learned how to deliver it off by heart.

---

1 RESILIENCE
2 REACH
3 RAPPORT

4 Rules

I don't know about you, but I've wasted hours in internal meetings. They rarely started on time and if they did, the absence of an agenda, the lack of a chairperson and a total disrespect for the fundamental principles of human kindness typically resulted in a free-for-all. They can be hideous corporate gatherings where you lose hours, lose the plot and occasionally lose your rag.

There are some upsides to having meetings at work. You get to look important, you can create the impression of doing stuff without actually doing it, you get to take credit for other people's ideas – you can even throw people who aren't at the meeting under the bus and you get to do all that in work time and be paid for it!

Joking aside, take my advice: never agree to attend a meeting unless there is an agenda, with timings agreed, and a chairperson to control both.

Whether we like it or not, if our objectives in life are to avoid chaos, limit stress and have a successful outcome, then we need guidelines or a set of rules. And the most essential time for rules to be put in place in our sales process is at the start of a meaningful sales conversation, directly after we've built rapport.

We need rules in the selling environment because selling is a contact sport. There are different agendas, multiple people, contrasting personalities and a boatload of emotions in play. If we aren't able to manage these in a respectful and disciplined way, frankly, we run the risk of getting shafted.

"It protects me from the time-wasters!"

Put crudely, having a set of rules is like wearing a sales condom. It's essential for protecting prospects from salespeople and salespeople from prospects. We need boundaries to manage how we interact with a prospect, but also to ensure that we do the right things before and after that conversation, too.

What rules a customer's head?

Admit it. You lie to salespeople!

Don't tell me you haven't told a sales assistant in a shop that you're 'just looking' when they come over and ask if you need any help. We've all done that. We've been doing it for years. We've had to, because of that widely held belief that salespeople are there to manipulate us into buying things we don't want. But buyers have their own tactics, which you need to be aware of.

Buyer rule one: Stay safe

What rules a customer's head when they come into contact with a salesperson is the need to stay safe. It's as if they need to hold some magical 'sales shield' up to protect them, except that shield is a verbal one and it comes in the form of being less accommodating with the truth.

This problem then compounds itself if the salesperson isn't aware of this rule, takes the prospect's response at face value and doesn't have the skill and confidence to push back and identify the buyer's true reasons for being there. This leads to prescription before diagnosis, which most would agree is poor sales practice.

Buyer rule two: Get something for nothing

The second thing to rule a buyer's head is looking for opportunities to get something for nothing – heck, everyone likes free stuff, right? In the past, I have been asked for (and given) more free hours of advice than I care to mention to corporate buyers. I've completed time-consuming and complex spreadsheets to analyse cost by product mix, and have provided countless proposals and quotations that never got a thank you, let alone an order (more about these in chapter nine).

Working collaboratively with buyers to bring about a meaningful sales discussion that leads to a sale makes sense. But don't be surprised if you get nothing in return for this 'free help', especially if you don't protect it with some rules of your own.

Buyer rule three: Always negotiate

Once a buyer has received their 'free gift', their third rule kicks in: always negotiate. What's not to like about getting free stuff from a salesperson and then asking for and receiving a discount on your first purchase?

Because buyer rules have been in place ever since selling began, it's normal for salespeople to be told that their price is 'too expensive' and for them to rectify the problem by reducing it, under the illusion that this is negotiation. I like to call it 'insanity'.

Negotiation isn't selling. In fact, it's the total opposite. When we sell, we reassure the buyer that the price they're paying is justified. In negotiation, there's a lack of justification so price becomes *the* factor and the main event. Then it's about conceding ground and trying not to give away more than you need to, to keep the deal alive. That's assuming, of course, that buyer rule number four hasn't already happened…

Buyer rule four: Go quiet

Once a buyer has been offered your best and lowest price, they have no need for you anymore, so they deploy rule four – radio silence. Typically, this happens while they're showing your discounted price to their current supplier, waiting for them to reduce theirs, too. Ninety-nine times out of a hundred, you'll never hear from the buyer again and you're left trying to figure out why the dead cert you added to your CRM just went ghost.

Now you know these four 'rules', learn them and learn how to avoid becoming a victim of them. The following chapters will give you everything you need to do this, so read on.

Define your leads

When you receive an approach or a lead, it's important to follow the rules and treat each one with careful consideration from the outset. Now is not the time to put out the bunting or update the CRM, now is the time to be realistic and establish whether this lead could convert into a sale or not. But are they a lead, a suspect or a prospect? Here are some definitions that should help you work that out:

- **Lead** – You have a name and contact details only, possibly as a result of someone engaging with your PFPs. But right at this moment, there is no way you can treat this as anything more than a business card you found on the back seat of an Uber. **Likely to buy status: 0%**

- **Suspect** – Anyone who you've been able to have a conversation with. You may have come across them at one of those appalling networking events you keep promising yourself you won't go to again. If you're really lucky, you've managed to share your social pitch with them and they smiled! **Likely to buy status: 0%**

- **Prospect** – They fit your ICP and they're willing to offer their time to help you get in front of all of the right people, where you'll establish who ultimately holds the cash and who makes the buyer decision. **Likely to buy status: 25%**

- **Qualified prospect** – A prospect who has overall ownership of the decision-making process and has given you a verbal commitment that they're hell-bent on solving their problem within an acceptable timeframe that works for you both. **Likely to buy status: 50%**

- **Closeable prospect** – A qualified prospect who has answered positively all of your questions, has satisfied you that they are 100% committed to solving their problem, and would do so with a product that looks just like yours. **Likely to buy status: 75%**

Recognising that our various prospects conform to certain rules and that each has a clear probability or 'likely to buy' status allows us to avoid looking like a sales novice, or an 'order-taker'.

If you want to avoid unnecessary heat from the C-Suite and want realistic information in your CRM rather than fiction, be acutely aware of the rules around what qualifies someone who'll buy what you sell.

Be prepared

This is the part of the book where you may be expecting me to give you some trite nonsense about perfect planning or not starting a journey without activating your satnav. Let's be honest, you've heard it all before and (like me) may feel like vomiting every time you see some self-righteous, self-appointed motivational speaker post a picture of someone on a mountain pointing to the stars saying, 'Failing to prepare is preparing to fail.' Give me strength!

But the truth is that my least effective sales calls almost always took place when I hadn't prepared well enough beforehand. I could argue that in the late 1990s, when I first started in corporate B2B sales, the internet wasn't what it is today and finding information about a prospect was like searching for gold dust.

It was nothing like we have today. We have instant access to unlimited information in milliseconds. There is absolutely no excuse for not knowing almost everything you need to know about your prospect before you engage with them. Those who don't research and gather data in advance – or choose not to – are guilty of not only wasting their employer's time and money, but their prospect's, too.

You might think that 'So, how's business?' is a good question, but the reality is, you should already know before you ask that. As we'll cover in the next chapter, the days of asking blatantly obvious questions are over if you want to be an outstanding sales professional rather than a mere order-taker.

Let's take a look at some of the things we could research in advance to form the basis of a pre-call plan that can help us increase the chances of converting a prospect into a qualified one.

1. **The basics** – Start with good housekeeping, the basic things you need to know to have your sales conversation. It makes sense to capture the names and roles of the attendees. The date and venue are also important. Decide if this is a meeting with a prospect or an existing customer.

2. **Psychography** – Think back to the ICP exercise in chapter two. Do you know what their personality type is? This will help with your communication style. If you're not sure how to establish this, look up DISC® and research communication styles.

3. **Social engineering** – Check out their website and LinkedIn profile and see if they engage online, and if so how they engage, and with what content. This will help with building up their psychographic profile. While you're there, look at how they've created their profile and try mapping out their colleagues, as some of these may be stakeholders in future purchasing decisions.

4. **Your key objectives** – Set out your aims for the call. Three is an ideal number. Consider sorting

them into (a) primary – what you *must* achieve at the meeting, (b) secondary – what you would *like* to achieve and (c) tertiary – what would be a good *consolation* prize if you don't get the first two.

5. **Your key questions** – Your online research should have boxed off the fruitless 'How's business?', 'How many people work here?' and 'What's your annual revenue?' type questions. So now think instead about which deep and meaningful questions you could ask that will really open up the conversation.

6. **Their key questions** – Have a think about what they might ask you. Why wouldn't they want the answers to questions like 'Why is it so expensive?', 'How come you know so much about me?' and – my particular favourite – 'You're really good. Why aren't our salespeople as good as you?'

7. **Your desired outcome** – as Yogi Berra, the famous New York Yankees baseball player and coach said, 'If you don't know where you are going, you'll end up someplace else.' Listing what you ultimately want to achieve allows you to always bring the conversation back in line with the direction in which you want to travel.

Having a pre-call plan with topics like this researched in advance not only gives you a map or agenda to refer to, but this knowledge works wonders for your self-belief and mental resilience. Go one stage further and rehearse the questions and role play the meeting with your colleagues and you'll walk into your sales call with the indisputable confidence that every ultra-high-performing sales professional has.

The Rules of Engagement

Picture the scene. You meet someone at a trade show and they're engaged by your empathetic and respect-fully curious approach. They're willing to admit that they have had the problems you describe in your social pitch and have shared a couple of others that are currently giving them sleepless nights. They've sampled some of your PFPs and that's steered them towards signing up for your free thirty-minute one-to-one 'discovery' call.

Here's where rules really come into their own. This set of principles that I call the 'Rules of Engagement' have transformed my own results and those of my clients more than anything else I teach. Don't be fooled by their simplicity or put off by the mild chutzpa associated with delivering the Rules of Engagement, just deliver them at the start of every scheduled pitch or meeting and I guarantee you'll transform your results, too.

Rule one: Make sure they know why they're meeting you

At the start of the call, despite the fact that it's all about them, you are going to assume the role of chairperson and take control. Why wouldn't you? You've prepared well, you have your pre-call plan and you know exactly why you've allocated time in your schedule to meet. The question is, do they? Clarifying this upfront ensures there's total transparency between buyer and seller from the off and if they state this first, you'll know what their agenda is. You could say, 'Claire, thanks for deciding to reach out. Just so I'm clear that we're both on the same page, do you want to let me know why you've jumped on the call with me today?'

Rule two: Give yourself enough time to discuss things

Next, you need to make sure that the time you've allocated in your busy schedule has been worth your while. Agree the discussion time with your prospect – enough to say everything you both need to. You could say, 'Claire, when we confirmed today's meeting on email, we agreed to meet for thirty minutes. Are you still OK to stick with that time today?'

What this does is place a value on your time. Anything other than a confirmation from your prospect might suggest a lack of commitment.

Rule three: Share your objectives

Now that you have agreed why you're talking and how long you've got, you need to lay out the agenda. Share your three objectives from your pre-call plan. For example, 'Claire, to ensure that I can deliver the reason why you're on the call, I've got three objectives:

1. I'd like your permission to ask you some questions so I can understand more about the problem you want help with. Is that OK?

2. I'd like you and I to find and agree what the root cause or causes are behind that problem.

3. Finally, if it looks like there's a fit, I'd like us to agree the next suitable step – does that sound fair?'

This rule creates even more transparency and helps the prospect lower their 'sales shield'. You're basically saying, 'My intentions are honourable. There's nothing up my sleeve. I mean you no harm.' Clearly, they're the star of this show, so we now need to ask them what they want to discuss.

Rule four: Ask them what their objectives are

'So, how about you, Claire? What are your objectives?'

I'll be honest with you – I can count on one hand the number of times a prospect has given me an objective of their own. Maybe it's because they didn't go in with a pre-call plan. Or they could have been comfortable with the way the conversation was going. In my experience, most simply said, 'Your objectives work for me.' That endorsement right there paves the way for the fifth and final rule.

Rule five: Agree what success looks like for the prospect

In other words, close at the start. You could ask, 'OK, Claire, what must happen by the time we finish to allow you to say that meeting with me today was a worthwhile use of your time?'

Only a classically trained salesperson insists on this rule and consequently, most prospects will have never been asked it and won't have prepared to answer it. What you'll essentially get here is their honest response, no BS. Decide to deliver what they tell you, and you're essentially guaranteeing your own success by giving them theirs.

The Rules of Engagement place you in control of the sales conversation. This is essential if you're to protect both yourself and your time. You'll protect your prospect, too. By using transparent communication and agreeing at the start what you both want to happen at the end, you are placing them at the heart of the movie, making them the star and you the director. But remember, at this stage of the sales process, you still have no certainty that the person in front of you will buy what you're selling.

What does all this mean for the sales process?

We've seen that prospects and customers can sometimes behave irrationally, but do so for rational reasons. They distort the truth not to be awkward, but from a defence mechanism against being manipulated – because no one likes that.

We've reminded ourselves that buyers like a deal and that negotiation, as much as I strive to avoid it, does happen. Our role as sales professionals is to protect our price and avoid entering into a negotiation unless it's a last resort.

We've looked at the various status levels that apply when qualifying a prospect and that even when we're in a discussion with a 'closeable prospect', they're still only 75% likely to buy – the deal isn't done until they sign on the dotted line.

We've covered a framework for a pre-call plan, so that we are as prepared as we can be going into a sales call and we know how to control the discussion so that both parties get what they want.

In the next chapter, we'll find out why everything you've read so far is pointless if the person in front of you doesn't have one of two things.

But before we head there...

WHAT'S ONE THING YOU COULD DO TODAY?

Introduce a pre-call plan as a compulsory part of your sales process. Time investing in preparation will pay back double. It will improve your mindset and attitude knowing that you can handle anything that comes your way and upping the quality of your prepared questions will elicit more informative answers.

---

5 Reason

My entry into the world of sales was a late one compared to some. No standing at the end of the street selling refreshing homemade Kool-Aid to thirsty passers-by at the age of four for me. I've always been slightly sceptical of the self-proclaimed 'lemonade brigade' if I'm honest. I don't for a minute doubt it happened, but without any mention of 'Cost of Sales' or EBITDA, I can't take these 'sales' stories seriously, I'm afraid.

Instead, my first foray into arguably the oldest profession known to man, was upon leaving school aged sixteen. I resisted the temptation to head off to university and opted to take a job working in a shoe shop in the fine city of Norwich, UK.

Allow me to share with you what happened in my first week at work – it will help explain a great deal about the importance of buyer–seller communication. At the end of this chapter, you will have total clarity behind the reasons why people do and don't buy and some of the mistakes that contribute to the latter.

You'll discover, too, that there are no dark arts or 'secret sauce' required to be good at selling and that those who claim there are simply overcomplicate a logical and predictable process. Their activities might sound intriguing but in reality bring nothing new when you explore further.

Let me take you back to my world in England in 1984...

Don't sell shoes, sell shoe-trees

I arrived for work on my first day and was greeted at the door by Mr Barker. He was a slim, somewhat charismatic chap and a Scouser (born in Liverpool) with an engaging tone to his words. He quickly made me feel at home, gave me a tour of the shop and introduced me to the other members of staff.

He then explained what was expected of me in my new sales role: 'Matt, here's how we do things around here. Your job is not to sell shoes.' Despite my junior years, I'd learned enough in life to know that his words, my understanding of the job and my 'shoe sales assistant' badge didn't tally.

Mr Barker's explanation was concise. 'Matt, when people walk into a shoe shop, they've already decided they want to buy a pair of shoes – that work is done, I don't need you to duplicate it.' It took me a few seconds and while I was hoping I could, it was difficult to disagree with his logic.

'Of course, you're going to help them decide which pair and then relieve them of their money,' he said, 'but the sale has already taken place before they walked in the store, so your job therefore is slightly different. I want you to sell people something they don't yet know they need.'

His eyes left me momentarily as he pointed to the rack of polish, brushes and laces next to the till and sighed. Fixing his gaze on me once again, he said, 'Your job isn't to sell shoes, it's to sell shoe-trees.'

And with that, he wished me good luck and disappeared, leaving me alone in the shop, with a couple of customers, a store cupboard packed full of shoe-trees and an element of trepidation about what was to happen next.

During that first week, I must have asked more than two hundred customers if they wanted to buy a pair of shoe-trees. The sum total of sales in exchange for my efforts was just one, to a particularly demanding and aggressive old woman who tried to haggle me down on price. And despite the fact that I stood my ground and resisted my mother's request for a discount, it was clear that this selling thing was harder than I'd first thought.

Fearing the worst, when Mr Barker visited me on the shop floor at the end of the week, I was surprised at his response. Rather than frustration on his part, there was a sense of relief. In place of despair, there was joy.

'Congratulations, Matt – you've cracked it!' he said with a smile on his face. 'In less than a week, you've discovered what most salespeople fail to work out in a lifetime.' Somewhat grateful that I still appeared to be employed and sensing that if there was a good time to ask a foolish question, this was it, I pushed back. 'Sorry, Mr Barker, I'm not being funny, but are you feeling OK?'

What Mr Barker went on to explain not only made total sense to me all those years ago, but his advice continues to sit at the core of how I sell today:

- First, he explained that **people buy for their reasons not mine**. The prospect is the star of the show, not the salesperson or their product.

- Next, he told me that **people only buy one of two things**: a solution to a problem or an improvement to something that already exists. No problem, no sale.

- Finally, off the back of those two points, he reminded me of the classic Jeffrey Gitomer concept, that **people don't like to be sold to, but they love to buy**.[7] Selling your product or service isn't something you do at or to people, it's something you do *with and for* people.

Knowns, unknown knowns and unknown unknowns

Armed with this wisdom and still apparently employed, I started to feel better about my first week sales faux pas and was keen to learn more from Mr Barker. He provided me with three more absolute knowledge bombs back in 1984 and I'm going to link them to today's sales world so you can see how they've stood the test of time and why they're so important if we are to convert more leads into sales.

Everybody knows what they know

When you receive a lead from a prospect, they will already have a desire to buy what you sell. In the famous 'Always Be Closing' scene in the classic film *Glengarry Glen Ross*, Alec Baldwin's character, Blake, reminds us that, 'People don't walk onto a car lot

---

7   www.gitomer.com/people-dont-like-to-be-sold-but-they-love-to-buy

unless they want to buy [a car].' When people come into a shoe shop, they know they are looking for shoes and they know what shoe size they are, because everybody knows what they know.

It's exactly the same with your prospects. They're looking to enquire, find out about, maybe even buy what you sell. By the same logic, they also know a fair amount about your product or service because you kindly give them a huge amount of information via your website, your social media posts and your marketing offers.

Though regarded today as a bit of a myth, it's easy to see how the often-quoted statistic that 70% of the buyer's journey is completed before a buyer even reaches out to a salesperson became sales gospel. It may even still carry some credence today.

We must accept that there is so much information at their disposal, perhaps the hardest thing about B2B selling today is that customers don't need you the way they used to. Whether it's off the back of their own research conducted by experienced procurement teams or purchasing consultants armed with troves of data, companies can readily define what they believe to be their own solution for themselves.

But this gives you even more reason to consider and apply what we covered in chapter two, so you can infiltrate the 70% earlier and join the conversation going on inside your prospect's head.

EVERYBODY KNOWS WHAT THEY KNOW – FOLLOW-UP QUESTIONS

Q: Put yourself in your prospect's shoes and research yourself – what do you find?
Q: If you Google yourself, what comes up?
Q: When you look at your website, does it clearly demonstrate it's for your ICP?

Everybody knows what they don't know

If we allow ourselves to delve into the logical yet complex world of systems thinking, we'll establish that when we ask a prospect what they want, we'll get a mix of their needs, their expectations and their suggested solutions. But more often than not, these are expressed in an inconsistent and ambiguous fashion.

What's also missing (according to the lab coats in the systems thinking world) is a full set of customer requirements – the things they're required to do to solve the problem. The best we can expect for them to have completed is just 30%. This much is obvious, because if they knew what 100% of their requirements were, they wouldn't need you.

This 'requirement gap' is the reason why people came into the shoe shop. They knew they wanted a pair of shoes and while they had a rough idea, they didn't know the exact style or how much they would spend to get them.

That 70% gap is why prospects need our help. Our job as salespeople is to understand their needs, recognise their expectations and sometimes help them see that their original solutions aren't always the best ones. A good example of this in my world is helping convince a client who's competing on price, that they *don't* need negotiation training!

We must be certain that we can help our customers solve their problem, by completing their missing 70% with our solution, before deciding if we actually want to.

**EVERYBODY KNOWS WHAT THEY DON'T KNOW –
FOLLOW-UP QUESTIONS**

Q: Head back to your website. Is the problem you solve clearly identifiable?

Q: Do you incorporate the problems you solve in your PFPs?

Q: Like the Audit (chapter two), do you have a way to help your prospect diagnose what their problem is, so they can see a way forward?

Nobody knows what they don't know

This final piece of advice from Mr Barker is probably the hardest to grasp, but will produce the greatest impact on your conversion rate once you do. The simplest way to explain it is to ask you to imagine you're down the pub playing a game of darts. It's your turn and you're aiming your first throw at the bullseye. Fifty points!

Let's imagine that this tiny segment in the middle of the board represents everything you know you know. Work with me on this, I'm sure you know lots of stuff, but I want you to create a visual representation in your mind. The red bullseye is everything you've ever learned at school, university, classroom training courses, online programmes, etc.

If you then look at the green segment which surrounds the bullseye, called the outer bull (worth twenty-five points), this represents everything you know that you don't know. For example, if you don't know which orange came first, the colour or the fruit, that's there. Equally, if you don't know who put the alphabet in alphabetical order and had never even thought of that until now, then that's there, too – make sense?

Outside these two segments, every other segment on the dart board is everything you don't yet know even exists. I can't give you any examples, because I've no idea myself what's out there, but it is and some of it could be really useful to know. I'd be willing to invest in any of that unknown information if it helped grow my sales, wouldn't you?

"Just need double 'everything I don't know' to finish!"

Here's the thing – you will already know a lot of information in your customer's 'unknown, unknown' segments and some of that could be really useful for them to discover. You know about their market, because you sell into it. You know about future trends that could impact that market, because you study and research it. You understand what your customer's customer is thinking, because you're connected and engage with many of them on LinkedIn and you talk to them regularly.

**NOBODY KNOWS WHAT THEY DON'T KNOW –
FOLLOW-UP QUESTIONS**

Q: What information do you have or could find that
would be of real value to your prospects and
customers?

Q: How could you build this into your eco-system of
PFPs to create early engagement?

Q: Why wouldn't you want to build mining this priceless
'unknown, unknown' information into your existing
customer retention activity?

Questions are the answer

So far in this chapter, other than the fact we've established I was hopeless at selling shoe-trees, you now
know that your prospects are already armed with
loads of information about your product, service and
you, before they make contact. And you also know
that there's a bunch of really useful information – that
you have – that could be really useful for them if they
found out about it.

The great news for salespeople is that this is not only
true for all our customers, regardless of what we're
selling, but we also have the ability to significantly
influence them if we're willing to do the work. If
we do, we'll not only convert more prospects into

customers, we'll convert them into lifelong customers and even 'raving fans' as Ken Blanchard refers to them in his bestselling book of the same name.[8]

To do this, we have to link back to chapter three, where we learned how to develop sales behaviour built on empathy. You'll recall it starts with adopting an attitude which is open-minded and curious about your prospect's plight.

Thinking this way will naturally steer you towards asking questions to uncover more information – insightful, challenging and stunning questions which catapult the conversation into the world of knowns, unknowns and unknown unknowns.

The phrase 'permission-based selling' has been around for years, but it's flawed. Think about it – what do you think your results would be like if you spent your prospecting time asking this: 'Hey, friend. Could you give me the thumbs-up to sell you something?' Probably not great.

Try flipping it to 'permission-based helping'. Instead of asking permission to sell, ask for permission to help your prospect buy. To do this, you must start by asking one of the best sales questions ever:

---

8   K Blanchard and S Bowles, *Raving Fans: A revolutionary approach to customer service* (Harper, 2011)

'For me to really see things from your perspective, Paul, I need your permission to ask you some questions. Is that OK with you?'

This is such a powerful question to ask and almost always gets rewarded with a 'Yes'. It opens up endless possibilities for taking your prospect on a journey, a journey that will end with them accepting that they have a problem – a real one that won't solve itself and that they would like you to help them solve. The outcome will be right for them, but is one that you control.

Asking the right questions to achieve this joint goal doesn't just happen. You need a bunch of outstanding questions and you need to learn them so that they become instinctive. This means you know when and why you're asking them. We'll look in depth at what the right questions are to ask, but let's conclude this chapter with some basic principles for asking questions:

1. **Plan in advance** – Every prospect will have different problems, needs and desires, so do your research (pre-call plan) and list the questions that will uncover them.

2. **Use the Pareto principle** – Most salespeople aren't scared of talking, but you'll need to get your prospect doing just that if you want to

discover what they know and don't know. Apply the 80/20 rule and aim to ask questions 20% of the time and for your prospect to spend 80% of the time answering them.

3. **Avoid waste** – With so little time, you cannot waste it by asking crap questions. These are ones you could have asked yourself and found out prior to the call. Questions about number of employees, revenue, how long your prospect has worked there are all poor ones – don't ask them. The answers to those will place you no further forward in the sales process.

4. **Positively challenge** – You've got permission, so don't hold back. The problem they think they have is almost never the true problem, so probe. Ask 'Why?' again and again until you uncover the genuine root cause. They'll thank you for it. Trust me, I've saved prospects thousands by asking why they think they needed pointless negotiation training!

5. **Listen well** – I'm no neuro-linguistic programming expert, but I know that seeking out body language clues is a complex task, all that 'eyes up and left' stuff is a bit too ninja-like for me. But listening is easy. If you don't hear what you want, ask a better question. If you hear what you want, ask another one like that.

6. **Get to the sweet spot answers** – These are the ones you must strive to receive. When a prospect

says 'Great question' or better still, 'Wow, no one's ever asked me that question before', you'll know you've hit the sweet spot. When they're giving answers like this, they know the person in front of them is a professional, someone who genuinely cares and someone they'll respect.

What does all this mean for the sales process?

We know that prospects will research us extensively before they reach out to meet us, which reinforces the importance of creating a personal brand and plenty of easy-to-access content for them to consume.

We've explored the fact that sometimes the problem a prospect comes to us with isn't the true problem and that we have to probe a little deeper.

We know that asking great questions is the way to uncover the deeper problem and to do this properly, we need their permission. With this, you have a green light to move the sales process to the next phase: commitment.

Turn the page and let's look at how we get a prospect to commit all-in and get us closer to converting them into a customer.

But before you do…

WHAT'S ONE THING YOU COULD DO TODAY?

Research ways to improve your listening skills. You'll find plenty of free information on the internet, but consider investing in some online training. You'll be surprised how much you can learn for a relatively small investment.

6 Resource

One of the biggest mistakes people make when selling is to assume that your customer is actually able to buy from you. Answer me this: how many times have you enjoyed a positive conversation with someone who appears genuinely interested in what you're offering, only to find that when you get to the fun bit – the bit where they're supposed to say, 'I'm in! Where do I sign?' – they don't?

Much of my early corporate sales career was plagued with false starts like this. At the time, I naively assumed it was just the way it was in selling. You win some, you lose some. Well, that's partly true. Not every opportunity you find will convert into a sale, but every one that doesn't can be avoided long before it robs you of too much time and resource.

Cast your mind back to chapter four and remind your-self that even a closeable prospect only carries a 75% 'likely to buy' status. And they're only one step away from being closed.

Many salespeople I meet (including myself during my corporate career in the early 2000s), go about their business with the opposite approach, one of total accommodation for anyone who looks remotely like a prospect. There could be underlying psychological reasons for this naivety, but much of the time it comes down the salesperson's deep-rooted fear of hearing the word 'No'. Hence, they go out of their way to avoid the conflict associated with getting one.

The infamous sales mantra 'know, like and trust' has a lot to answer for, in my opinion. While 'know' and 'trust' are clearly non-negotiable, the 'like' element is, at best, optional and in certain cases, unhelpful.

The danger with this obsession with needing to be liked is obvious. Not only will you spend time with people who are just wrong for your business, you'll fill up your pipeline with fiction. You'll spend what time you have left split between avoiding the weekly CRM update meeting with your boss and activating your lifetime membership to your prospect's voice-mail and those, my friend, are two grim activities.

I'm not suggesting for a moment that you should be arrogant or pushy. Behaviours like those are reserved

for the immature and uneducated in the sales industry. But I *am* asking you to consider a more cautious
approach. I'd like you to consider being 'respectfully
sceptical'.

Let's find out what this means and how it can serve
us.

The C-word

Traditional selling focuses on drawing qualified prospects into a funnel that then leads to a sales process.
What you've discovered in the chapters so far is the
need to focus on disqualifying the non-prospects
before they reach the funnel. It's about becoming
adept at identifying the wrong prospects, even those
who could be classed as the right ones but, crucially,
don't demonstrate the C-word – commitment.

Look up the word 'commitment' and it will dish up
a number of definitions like 'being dedicated to the
cause' or 'an obligation that restricts freedom of action'.
These are exactly the behaviours your prospect needs
to demonstrate when they're engaging with you. I like
to use the following acronym to explain it:

- C – They're **committed** because:

- W – They **want** to change and have told you so,
  explicitly.

- **O** – They've **organised** themselves so they're able to take action.

- **R** – They'll **realign** their business to implement your solution.

- **D** – They've **decided** now is the time to take action.

Being committed to buy what you sell requires a prospect to have a number of resources at their disposal. Let me explain what I mean. Imagine you were off to meet your friends for a few drinks at the pub. You'd need cash, you'd need to book a taxi, you'd need to look your best, so you'd need to have your best outfit clean, ironed and ready to go. You'd need a pub to meet in and a time to meet… you get the idea.

All of these things are resources and they all need to be in place for you to execute the perfect night out. If you had them all, you'd be fully prepped and totally committed to making merry with your mates. Leave one out and while you still might go out, would your evening promise to be as much fun if you had to walk there and back? Leave out a couple of the requirements and your commitment would waver and you'd start to doubt if it was worth bothering going out at all.

It's the same in sales. Outside of disqualifying prospects who don't fit your ICP, ensuring those who do are fully committed is probably the single most important contributor to converting more leads into sales. If you get really good at gaining commitment from prospects, then your deal-time and conversion rate will start to head in totally opposite, positive directions.

'So, what are the resources that prospects need to have if they're going to be committed to buy?' I hear you cry. Well, there are three non-tangible resources, ie things you can feel, and three tangible resources, ie things you can touch. Let's start with the non-tangible.

Partnership

A committed prospect will recognise that they have the problem, not you, and in order for them to solve it, they need your help. Adopting a working relationship that's both professional and collaborative by nature will give you both the best possible chance of success. You need your prospect to act like a partner, not a purchaser.

Open-mindedness

Let's face it, your prospect is coming to you with what they believe is the right problem, the thing they know they don't know how to solve. You need to help them see that there's real value for them if they commit to exploration, investigation and new ideas. Just like a parachute, a mind works best when it's open.

Movement

Your mind is a wonderful thing – it can see into the future. Try it! Helping your prospect visualise life after you've helped them offers them the chance to commit to take action with you to make this vision reality. Without this, it's just 'jam tomorrow' – get them to commit to forward movement with you.

And now for the tangible resources they need.

Capacity

You need your prospect's commitment to allocate time to meet regularly, to respond to email and video calls, and to make new time available in their diary for follow-up. By being transparent and explaining at the beginning just how much time they'll need to commit avoids surprises and allows them to plan ahead.

Stakeholders

The person in front of you may not be a final decision-maker, but they should be able to grant you access to those that are. This critical commitment to putting you in front of the stakeholders needs to happen as soon as possible. Leave it too long and those people will resent not being involved earlier. Building a collaborative relationship with the decision-makers also allows you to take everyone along together.

Correction

There will be times when your offer won't be received with a standing ovation. Some things in your proposal may not work. Unless you get their commitment to correct these things, you could lose a deal over some minor issue which could have been easily adjusted had you known about it. Get them to agree to this resource and it's essentially your deal to lose.

Make securing these resources your first priority *before* you get to the main event of talking about your product or service and I'll guarantee you'll have a productive and meaningful sales conversation. You'll also avoid wasting your valuable time with people who might look like prospects, but who don't have what it takes to buy from you.

The budget question

We've touched on the point about the obsession many salespeople have for needing to be liked, the ego-state which craves being massaged with nods of approval from prospects and a desire to hear 'Yes' rather than 'No'.

Don't misunderstand me, hearing a 'Yes' at the right time is essential, especially when the whole sale is predicated on getting a big fat one when we go for the close. But continuously trying to please a prospect can seriously damage your ability to convert them into customers.

The 'prospect pleaser' mindset is an unhealthy one at the best of times, but when it comes to asking for cash, it's a killer. One of the most important resources our prospects must have is budget – no cash, no sale. But there's something about money that gets even the most experienced sales professional a tad twitchy.

Asking if your prospect has the funds should be a no-brainer. It's better to find out if they haven't got any budget early on rather than later. But my guess is there'll have been times when you've either forgotten to ask or have avoided asking, possibly so as not to derail what had been (up until then) a great conversation with lots of positives.

"No, budget's not a problem... I don't have any!"

The whole subject matter of 'budget' has been thrown into turmoil in recent years following the negative press that surrounds one of the original Holy Grails of selling, BANT.

BANT stands for Budget, Authority (to buy), Need and Timeline. Developed by IBM in the 1950s, BANT has always been regarded as the main lead qualification methodology to increase the probability of closing a deal with a prospect. It's lasted for over sixty years because it's concise, it's easy to remember and it's essentially a great approach to consider when qualifying a prospect.

But the days of seller-centricity are over. We have moved away from a time when the seller held all of the information and therefore controlled the sale to now, when the buyer has access to a near infinite amount of information. It's widely accepted that a buyer with time on their hands, a smartphone and a fair wind can probably find out all they need to know about your product and service and make a decision to buy without even speaking to you.

What we'll find when we move to the next chapter is that qualification now follows a buyer-centric methodology, as the sales process has become much more customer-oriented and value-driven. You might get away with following BANT with inexperienced prospects, but in the B2B complex sale environment, where buyers have probably attended more sales training than the sales people they meet, following BANT to the letter would probably get you kicked out of their office.

If you doubt this advice, think about this scenario: You're clothes shopping and the very first thing the sales assistant says to you is, 'Hi there. Do you have the money to buy that jacket?' Ouch!

The dilemma we face is that we must still establish if our prospect has the funds, but we need to find out in such a way that it brings value to the sales conversation. The classic 'So, what's your budget?' question is for amateurs, I'm afraid. I consigned that one to the rubbish bin years ago as soon as I realised it was both lazy and unsophisticated.

If there's an ideal way to establish budget, it's for the prospect to raise the question about money themselves. We'll look at how we can help them do this in the next chapter. But for now, let's just ask them like this: 'Lucy, I'm curious – this problem you've uncovered, have you already set aside funds to solve it yet or do you still need to build a business case?' Depending on the response, I might also follow up with, 'If you haven't, do you need help to build one?'

These presumptive, closed questions can only be answered with a 'Yes' or 'No' and they let Lucy know two important things: one, that money is a key factor for me and two, that I'm here to help her ask for some if she wants me to. These questions serve my needs and hold the prospect to account, so I'm still asking the 'What's your budget?' question, it just doesn't carry any threat.

Whether you opt to stick with BANT or align your sales process with one of the other lead qualification methodologies that exist, the key point I want to reinforce is that you must ensure you ask these fact-based qualification questions as soon as possible, and without jeopardising the trust that you're developing with your prospect.

Fail to do so and you run the risk of wasting your valuable time on deals that were never going to happen anyway. Better to get bad news about a lack of funds early, so you can shake them by the hand, acknowledge their honesty and move on to the next opportunity.

An inside job

As mentioned, we'll cover the full qualification questioning process in the next chapter. Let's assume the prospect has shifted to 'qualified', with a 50% 'likely to buy' status. It's time to start taking care of the person across the table and build that partnership we talked about. Get serious about supporting your prospect, aka your new Inside Salesperson with all the tools they need to close the sale for you.

When it comes to signing off the deal, there's a misconception that we have to tread on everyone else in the organisation and get to C-Suite. Go to the top of the business, find the CEO and sell to them, because they make the decisions and they write the cheques. In an ideal world, of course this would make a lot of sense, but tell me this – when did you ever sell in an ideal world?

When was the last time you got an appointment with a CEO? If you did, my guess is they probably didn't say, 'Great, let me get involved with all of the complexities of getting this deal over the line. Let me bang some dates into my diary now so I can be intrinsically involved at every meeting and be available for every follow-up call. I'm so up for this. I'm yours!'

In my experience, getting to C-Suite sounds great and should be your aim, but the best way to get there is through your Inside Salesperson. In my experience, C-Suite only show up at the start to kick the deal off and at the end to sign the cheque. And, quite frankly, they sign whatever's put in front of them if it comes with the endorsement of their staff, the people they trust most (and certainly more than they trust you).

At this point, your prospect becomes the CPO, the Chief Problem Officer. Not only do they have to solve the business problem they came to you with, they now have the problem of making sure it delivers in a way that pleases C-Suite. Otherwise, a potentially bigger problem will head their way!

This is where the educated sales professional comes into their own. Solving the business problem should be straightforward. Your product or service does that. But making sure it ticks all of the internal boxes does require more focus. There are a couple of key things at play that you must address:

1. **The 'What's in it for me?' factor** – in chapter one, we looked at the impact that personal responsibility has on results. You don't need to be a Jedi to accept that we have a deeper desire to achieve things if we know we're getting something in return. This is our 'What's in it for me?' factor and your CPO has one, too.

2. **Tip:** Establish what your CPO's 'What's in it for me?' factor is. Do they want recognition internally? Are they looking to gain promotion, and if so, will this deal help them achieve that? What can you do to bring their motivating factors into your deal?

3. **The decision-makers** – According to Gartner,[9] a typical buying group for a complex B2B solution involves six to ten decision-makers. It's not quite herding cats, but your job isn't as simple as just getting the CPO aligned with your message.

---

9   www.gartner.com/en/sales/insights/b2b-buying-journey

There's a whole roomful who need convincing that what you offer works for them, too.

4. **Tip:** As part of your pre-call plan (covered in chapter four), head over to LinkedIn and map out all the CPO's internal connections who warrant a place in the 'six to ten' club. You can then introduce these names in your qualification questions: 'Joe, while I was researching your company, I noticed that Rod, Jane and Freddy hold key roles, ones that would typically get involved with deals like ours. Will they be supporting you in the decision-making process and if so, how?'

Without these two critical resources, you cannot convince those who'll ultimately convince C-Suite. Success rests on respecting the CPO's role as the broker of the deal, keeping all of the decision-makers involved and, most importantly, getting them involved sooner rather than later. It's one thing knowing who calls the shots, but it's pointless if they resent the fact that they haven't been included earlier and decide to veto your offer. Sit down with your CPO and agree the best way to keep everyone involved, then make it happen.

Finally, it would be wise to put your empathy hat back on and ask yourself what knowledge the CPO would need to have to be able to sell on your behalf? Because as much as you might want to present your final proposal to their entire decision-making team, the likelihood is you won't. Unless you get lucky, all your focus must now switch to providing the CPO with the tools to do your job for you.

In the next chapter, we'll ask the questions that will build those tools. We'll establish the things we can provide for the CPO that can make selling less about the dark arts of neuro-linguistic programming or the sophisticated closing techniques from the 1980s and more about logic and payback.

What does all this mean for the sales process?

Despite human nature, we've established that you don't need to be liked to be good at selling. In fact, being a 'prospect pleaser' can negatively impact your ability to diagnose their problem correctly and that serves neither you nor them well.

We've also discovered that the C-word is a fundamental part of a salesperson's vocabulary and should be front and centre when communicating with prospects. Their commitment to buy needs to be established early and then cultivated throughout the conversation.

Understanding if they have the authority to buy and the funds to back it up are both obvious but often-neglected resources. As, too, are understanding your prospect's primary motivations and helping them achieve their aims. All these are critical to the success of every sale and are priorities for you right now.

Turn the page and let's get into the next chapter to find out that the secret to getting better answers lies in asking better questions.

But just before we get into all that...

WHAT'S ONE THING YOU COULD DO TODAY?

List all the things your Inside Salesperson would need to know and be convinced of about your product or service if they had to sell on your behalf. Bring this list into your sales conversations. The more they know, the easier it will be for them to satisfy their 'What's in it for me?' factor.

---

7 Reassure

It was almost four o'clock on that Friday afternoon back in 1984 and Mr Barker's advice that 'people only buy for their reasons' was still working its way around my sixteen-year-old brain. Little did I know, in the final hour before the store closed, Mr Barker was about to deliver a masterclass in selling that would amplify that golden rule and some of the others he'd told me.

Before I share what happened that day, I want you to know that while everything we've covered so far is intrinsic to the success of your sales process and your ability to convert prospects into customers, this chapter is without doubt the most important. By the time you've completed it, you will have total clarity around why people buy for their reasons and exactly what to do so they can reassure themselves that their reasons were justified.

The shop was almost empty, but a lady who had tried on a number of pairs of shoes finally approached the till and gestured her intent to buy. Mr Barker smiled at her, nodded as if to acknowledge her excellent choice and then got to work.

'Madam,' he said. 'Great choice, those are lovely shoes. Would it be OK with you if I asked you a couple of questions about why you bought them?' The lady was swift to grant him permission. 'Thank you. I'm curious, how often do you buy shoes, madam?'

The lady thought for a moment and then replied, 'Every other year. Shoes don't tend to last like they used to.'

Mr Barker smiled at her again and then looked up as if to search for the answer to some question going on inside his head. 'OK, so over the next twenty years, you'll probably buy ten pairs of shoes and invest something like £500 over that time?'

The lady nodded and replied, 'Yes, I suppose that feels about right. Quite a lot of money when you look at it like that, isn't it?' Mr Barker nodded and then continued with his questioning.

'Madam, when you wear these lovely new shoes in the rain, how will you get them dry?' The lady told Mr Barker about her airing cupboard, which she kept a constant twenty-three degree temperature and how wet shoes took no more than an hour to dry in there.

'Madam, would you be happy for me to share some free advice with you about wet shoes? I think it might help you in the future.' She agreed. He went on to explain that drying leather in accelerated temperatures causes the shoe to shrink and then tear when they are stretched to fit the next time they are worn – micro tears, mind, invisible to the naked eye.

He told her that the next time the 'stretched' shoes were worn in wet weather, the water would seep into the tears and start to degrade the leather, potentially shortening the life of the shoe.

The lady was surprised but grateful. 'My goodness,' she replied, 'I did not know that.' How could she have – nobody knows what they don't know. 'Thank you so much, I'm grateful for the advice. But what can I do about it?'

Mr Barker smiled confidently and explained how putting newspaper in wet shoes before drying would maintain the shape of the shoe and reduces the chances of the leather tearing. 'From experience, shoes taken care of this way will typically last twice as long as those that aren't. So rather than buying ten pairs over the next twenty years, you'll only buy five and save yourself £250.'

He went on to add, 'The newspaper should work OK, but if you want to really be certain and avoid getting ink from the newspaper inside your wet shoe and on your hands, why not invest just 10% of that saving in a pair of shoe-trees and guarantee it?'

Needless to say, the lady did just that and bought not one, but two pairs of shoe-trees, before thanking us both and leaving the shop one hundred pounds lighter but felling totally justified with her decision and her investment.

Dull, dangerous and downright delinquent

That true story is one I share when I speak at events. It's a great example of the importance of asking really good questions to educate and help reassure your prospect. When I think back to my years spent in the corporate B2B sales industry, from the years 1998 to 2013, the questions that I used to ask were quite dull, almost pointless.

By my calculations, based on asking five dull and pointless questions at every prospect or customer meeting, at an average of five meetings a week, over forty-six weeks a year, multiplied by fifteen years, I wasted more than seventeen thousand opportunities to progress the sale in a more meaningful and strategic way. What a waste! I daren't think how much money I left on the table!

Dull questions reek of a lack of preparation. They scream 'order-taker'. They could have been thought up on the back of a fag packet and asked by a monkey in a cheap suit. Dull questions lack motivation and without this, you can't progress and move forward. Here are some dull questions you should avoid asking:

- 'How long have you worked here?'
- 'What revenue did you make last year?'
- 'Who's that playing golf with you in the photo?'

Absolutely pointless, each and every one of them. Each brings no value to the conversation and all could have been discovered in advance through social engineering – even the golf one, just stalk their Instagram page. Dull questions, dull as dishwater.

Sometimes, dull ones don't appear dull until you dive a little deeper:

- 'Does that happen a lot?'
- 'Do you experience that often?'
- 'Was there much of an impact?'

At face value, they seem OK, but think about it. If a customer answered yes or no to those questions, you wouldn't really know much more than before you asked. There's nothing wrong with closed questions – in fact, some of the best questions to ask only get a one-word answer – but in these examples, you have to ask another if we're to get more information and keep the conversation moving in the right direction.

Mind you, better to waste your time with dull but safe ones, than make the mistake of asking dull and dangerous questions like 'How's business?'. Imagine how you'll feel when they reply, 'Crap! Sales are down. It's really tough. I sincerely hope you're not here to waste my time talking about anything other than your price?' Nothing's going to put you behind the eight ball quicker and derail your next move more than having to recover from a response like that!

And of course, everyone's favourite: 'Tell me, what keeps you awake at night?' The absolute signature move of the ill-prepared sales rep. Go on, try it. I'll be amazed if you don't get either 'The neighbour's cat' or 'Trying to work out at what depth pizza becomes deep-dish', or something equally non-sales-related.

"OK, apart from the neighbour's cat, what else keeps you awake at night?"

By getting this far in the book, you have more than enough tools to not be seen as an order-taker by your customers. By now, they'll be regarding you as a strategic partner and you'll be displaying the qualities that go with that accolade – namely, asking meaningful, sometimes challenging, but always intelligent questions. Or put another way, 'bright questions'.

Bright questions are well-thought through, advance the sale, and do so on your terms but at your prospect's request. Forgive the pun, but they bring the problem into the light, so it and the steps required to solve it can be clearly seen. Let's look at some examples and the ideal sequence for asking these using the acronym BRIGHT (Basics, Realise, Impact, Growth, Hijack, Transition).

B – Basics

You've always got to start with the basics. We've talked about BANT being pants, but it's the way BANT has been historically administered that creates the negative feeling towards it. No one is going enjoy going through a tick-box exercise of questions, but trust me, you'll enjoy getting to the end of the sale and finding out that they don't have the funds or authority to buy even less! Ask, 'Steve, can you help me understand the timings here? When had you planned to start taking advantage of a solution?'

R – Realise

Help them realise their problem won't solve itself. There's a reason why they reached out to you. If they could fix the problem themselves, they would have done so by now. Theirs is a cry for help, but it comes with a warning. Failure to help them see that solving their problem is what you do best simply gives them the option for you to hear the five worst words in sales: 'Let me think it over.'

You could say to them, 'Others we've helped also tried to solve it themselves, but it took longer than they thought and became quite costly for them. To eliminate the risk of that happening, under what circumstances would you allow me to solve it for you?'

I - Impact

Get them to see what the impact will be if they do nothing. Moving forward together is reliant on you switching from salesperson to fortune-teller to business expert. You've got to help the prospect see the error of their ways if they avoid taking action – this is no longer about sales, it's about business performance. Put a value on it for them. What would it cost them to do nothing?

Try this: 'I'm curious, Geoff. Let's pretend you just keep ignoring it and do nothing. Other than your own negative company performance, what impact will this have on your customers and your ability to retain them?'

G - Growth

What growth is on offer to them if they do take action and solve their problem? Now they're leaning in. That last part about cost has them focused. Now it's about using the 'law of attraction' to help them see the brave new world that could be theirs in the future. Again, this isn't about dark arts or Jedi mind tricks, this is simple business common sense. You could say, 'Let's just imagine this problem magically vanished today. What do you see happening to your sales growth plans over the next six, twelve and twenty-four months as a result, Neil?'

H – Hijack

What could hijack the deal from happening and how can this be avoided? At this stage, you can expect to see tangible signs of collaboration and it's deadly. Failing to tap the brakes here will result in them missing the pitfalls that exist in every sale. This is about identifying and mitigating business risk in advance. It takes an hour to list all the possible dangers – invest that time before moving on.

You could say, 'I know from painful experience that things don't always go to plan, Tom. So, take a couple of minutes and tell me what the possible internal barriers are that might restrict you from being able to progress with us as your supplier?'

T –Transition

What transition steps are required for your prospect to go from where they are today to achieving growth? With their confidence in you rising as a result of your insistence that they seek out a justifiable business case, you can revert back to sales tactics and begin to train them in how to sell to others. They'll ultimately be responsible for selling the deal internally, so getting your prospect to build a plan for what to do next is your job here. Transition questions will help you achieve this.

Try this: 'Have a think about this Sue – in your experience, what do you see as the next important steps we should both take over the next thirty days if we are to move forward successfully together?'

The key to being BRIGHT, is to maintain the sequence. Quite often, I observe salespeople who do all the hard work preparing a set of leading questions like these, but then rush through them, often skipping some of the steps. They miss out on providing the deep understanding that the prospect must achieve if they are to be convinced to make progress and ultimately buy what you're selling.

Being BRIGHT is all about asking questions whose answers achieve the commitment to proceed and doing so one step at a time. It's about asking, listening and leading your prospect to where they decide to go and being confident in your strategy so you can halt, back up and alter course should you need to. Bottom line, if you want to speed up the sale, slow down at the start.

Show them the money

In the next chapter, we're going to unpack the thorny subject of objections. But before we get there, I have one more tip about BRIGHT for you, which will considerably lessen or even eradicate objections to your sale. It's to make your BRIGHT questions not just bright but blinding. 'Excellent', 'superb' or 'outstanding' work too!

If we revisit the Impact and Growth questions from BRIGHT (the ones where we help our prospect calculate the size of their problem and the potential upside of removing it), to make these questions blinding, we can seek answers that build and jointly agree on a tangible financial impact of their problem.

This valuation is invaluable for a number of reasons. First, it helps the prospect clearly see that they have an issue to solve. Second, it can be used to build a business case to find the budget to solve it. And third, it moves the focus away from the price of your product or service and onto the total cost of their investment. They'll become less concerned about objecting to your price if they can see the solution delivers back more than they'll pay for it.

Let me show you a basic example from my world of sales training, so you can see how it plays out.

A sales director wants to train her team of twelve salespeople. Half of them are hitting quota, but these six could achieve another 20% given the right training and coaching support. A quarter of them are falling short by 15% and the other quarter by 25%. Each of the team looks after a £100,000 annual sales budget.

The sales director is a realist – she accepts that not everyone is able to achieve and exceed their budget, but she expects that an increase of 10% is more than possible.

Here's the maths.

The impact of doing nothing means her team are on track to miss budget this year by 10% or £120,000. But if she can support them to get their numbers up by 10%, she will reduce the gap between actual and budget to just 1% (£12,000).

We could build a case to suggest that while she didn't quite hit budget this year, she probably would next year, because the behaviour driven from training will repeat. A 10% improvement on this year's result would mean a further 8.9% growth (£106,800).

Therefore, the growth on offer if she decides to train her team is £108,000 this year and a further £106,800 next, totalling £214,800. Factor in another potential shortfall of £120,000 if she did nothing in the second year and the total opportunity for her adds up to a whopping £334,800, and that's just in the first two years!

Provided the total cost of the sales training didn't exceed £100,000, she'd not only treble her money in two years, she'd be safeguarding against losing staff by supporting their development and therefore saving on the additional costs associated with recruitment, neither of which are included in this scenario, but could be factored into your sales discussion.

I accept there are many variables at play and that this is a basic example, but it does give you a perspective on how Impact and Growth can become blinding at helping convert more leads into sales. The next time you get a chance to sit down with your prospect and 'do the maths', embrace it. If you show them the money and they can see the benefits for themselves, you'll not only reduce the chance of getting a price objection, you'll find asking for the sale becomes a whole lot easier. Heck, you'll probably find the prospect might even close the sale themselves!

What does all this mean for the sales process?

What we've achieved so far in this chapter will help your prospect reduce the risk they associate with parting with their cash and reassure them that what you're offering makes sense.

Your pre-call planning has allowed you to build a strategy that includes drawing up a set of relevant and highly impactful questions. The answers to these will give your prospect the knowledge and confidence to move forward with you.

In their eyes, you're not some sales rep who's rocked up to talk all about themselves and vomit their features and benefits everywhere. No, they see you as a provider of valuable and insightful information that's as much about making them more money than saving them less.

They're getting close to taking the decision to buy. Other than one or two concerns they might have and the need to bundle a deal together that they can sell internally, you're there.

Let's head into the next chapter and find out what sales objections are, why we get them and what we can do to avoid getting them at all.

But before you do that...

WHAT'S ONE THING YOU COULD DO TODAY?

Build your own unique set of BRIGHT questions – specific to your prospect's industry, market and problems. Share them with your boss or colleagues so that you are confident they're not just bright but blinding, asking them won't be a wasted opportunity and they'll advance your sales conversations forward.

8 Rectify

At the onset of the 2020 Coronavirus pandemic, my sales training business was severely challenged. Within two weeks, all my face-to-face training work was suspended and my pipeline had all but stalled. My ego took comfort in justifying the situation by reminding myself I wasn't alone. Every other training provider who delivered face-to-face training had a similar issue.

Once I'd got through the first week of trying to understand what my options were and after reaffirming with myself that I would do everything I could to avoid heading back to corporate employment, I moved into problem-solving mode. By the end of week two, I'd created a new one-to-one online coaching company, set up a new website, improved my online user experience to make it really easy for 'would-be' clients to gain access to me and started prospecting for leads.

In the first few days of week three, I had leads. One came in from a young sales professional who had been referred by someone who had experienced my training the previous year and got great results from it. I directed him, as I do all prospects, to my online disqualification scorecard. Within twenty-four hours, he'd qualified himself in by submitting his scores and we were on a Zoom call reviewing his results together.

Like so many sales professionals I meet for the first time, his scores told a different story from the one he'd come to me for help with. In his eyes, he was good at prospecting, building trust and questioning skills and was looking to reach the next level. But his conversion rate was just 58% and by his own admission, he was weak at dealing with prospect objections.

At the end of our session, he wanted to progress with some one-to-one coaching and we jointly established his expected return on his investment. He confirmed he was happy paying my fees and we agreed I'd send him the contract to sign within forty-eight hours.

The following day, I received the following email from him:

> 'I think for me to get the best out of this, I would like to wait until Covid-19 things calm down. This will also be a time of huge opportunity in the market. Fingers crossed in a month or two we can get something arranged.'

What happened? How did we go from 'sign me up' to 'press pause' in less than twenty-four hours? Did something happen to spook him? Why was he suddenly changing tack? Why has the classic 'Let me think it over' objection reared its ugly head? And how do I turn it around and handle it so he doesn't become another 'one that got away'?

Why buyers object

Contrary to popular sales folklore, salespeople don't create objections – they are already there. The reality is that every prospect brings their objections with them to the sales conversation. What salespeople do is create an environment for these objections to either exist or disappear.

They don't start out as objections, not the classic ones you and I have heard many times. Instead, they start as conscious thoughts, feeding off the negativity bias that exists within us all. They're thoughts designed with the best of intentions, protecting the prospect from the seller. Thoughts like, 'How do I make sure I don't pick the wrong supplier?', 'I hope I don't pay too much', and 'What happens if this doesn't work?'.

"I thought I'd bring my objections along with me!"

When we look at objections like this, they start to look different. They stop looking like things that could stop a sale and start to look more like something which could help someone avoid buying something they don't need and that's got to be a positive thing. No one sets out to buy the wrong solution.

In most cases, objections aren't really objections at all. Look up the word 'objection' and it will describe 'the action of challenging or disagreeing with something'. If I think back to the young sales professional and his decision to delay progressing with one-to-one coaching, he wasn't challenging me or disagreeing with what we'd agreed, he was simply raising his concern over the start time.

When someone objects to your price, they aren't disagreeing with it, they're voicing their concern that they cannot see the justification for what they're getting in return.

When someone tells you they need to think it over, they aren't disagreeing with your offer, they're letting you know that they don't see the urgency in taking action right now.

Objections aren't objections at all. They're just concerns.

Concerns that were always there, planted in the mind of the prospect. But rather than being resolved through the answers to our questions, we allowed them to manifest into verbalised concerns because we didn't reassure the prospect that they could let go of them.

When you reframe an objection so it becomes a concern, rather than be worried or nervous about receiving it, we should do the exact opposite. We should actually go and seek out concerns, knowing that if we can address all of them, there'll be no justifiable reason why our prospect won't buy!

As the salesperson, you're responsible for creating the environment for concerns to be either addressed or neglected. The prospect is the one who must resolve their concern because a prospect always believes what they tell themselves. Your job is to help them convince themselves they don't have any concerns after all.

Decode and disarm

One of the truths about objections is that, more often than not, what the prospect is saying and what they really mean are two different things. Sometimes this is simply down to the fact that the prospect doesn't want to offend by saying 'No'.

Delivering bad news to people feels uncomfortable. Given the choice between a truthful 'no' and dealing with the emotional baggage that follows, or a 'maybe', which prolongs the fantasy by being nice, most people will pick being nice all day long because it's the easier of the two.

But nice kills sales. It hides the truth and when we can't get to the truth, we can't help people. If we can't help people, we can't uncover their problems and no problem means no sale. Despite the fact that handling objections is one of the most popular sales skills I'm asked to deliver training on, it is rarely ever needed if you know how to sell.

Like me, you will get objections. But there is a distinct difference between those that come at this phase of the sales process, and those that presented themselves earlier, when we began the disqualifying phase.

Most would suggest that an objection about price is the most common objection of all. But surely this would only appear if you had given your prospect a price to consider in the first place? Yet here we are, eighty percent of the way through the book – and the sales process – and I've made no mention of how to or when to reveal your price.

If we think of other 'common' objections, like the infamous 'I'm busy right now', it's fair to say that you wouldn't hear that from a prospect who'd been through the stages covered by chapters five, six and seven (Reason, Resource and Reassure). If you did, then a simple, 'No problem, Jill. When's a good time to call you back?' would be all you'd need, with Jill's reply a 'Make sure you do'.

Let's take a look at four objections we often hear, which I often reframe as puzzles that need solving. These can be just as deadly as a price objection, but if we can decode them and find out what the prospect is really saying, we can disarm them and progress.

1. **Objection:** 'I'm busy right now, give me a call in a couple of months.'

2. **Decode:** 'I don't know who you are or what you want. So, given that you've made it really easy for me to avoid giving you my time now, I'll make it really easy for you to do it again in a couple of months and this whole merry-go-round can continue for eternity, if you like. Chances are, you won't call again anyway – most don't.'

3. **Disarm:** 'Sure, we could meet then. But before I waste your time, what will have changed on your side between now and then that would make meeting me in two months' time worth your while?'

This disarm sounds aggressive, but provided that you've delivered a valuable reason why they should meet with you, it sounds like it's not valuable enough for them. Why prolong the agony? Ask the obvious question or try humour and say, 'It's OK to tell me you're not interested, I hear it from my wife all the time. If you really want to say no, it's OK, I can take it.'

1. **Objection:** 'We've got that covered, thanks. We already have a supplier.'

2. **Decode:** 'My current supplier isn't the best, but you've provided me with no evidence that you'll be any better than them. Thanks, though – it's given me the kick up the backside I needed to find someone who really can deliver value and look after my business.'

3. **Disarm:** 'I appreciate that you have a supplier and it's probably fair to say that you're happy with them. But just out of curiosity, is there anything about them you would change if you could?'

This disarm positively challenges the prospect to decide if they are indeed happy with them or not. They either are and, in that case, you'll ask for a referral and move on or they're not, and they'll open the door for a conversation about their suppliers' weaknesses.

1. **Objection:** 'Can you send me some information?'

2. **Decode:** 'Let's play the game where I pretend to be interested and create the illusion whereby you're convinced I'm going to actually read whatever it is you send me. In reality, we both know I'm going to delete your email when it arrives and never see or hear from you again.'

3. **Disarm:** 'That's difficult without knowing more about the specific information you need. Look, I'm not here to waste your time and sending you the wrong information will do just that, so let's get together on Zoom for ten minutes and I'll answer every question you have and follow up with the exact information you need – does that sound fair?'

It's difficult to argue with logic here and so much of dealing with objections is about politely helping the prospect see that what they're saying makes no sense.

This disarm saves them time, and what sane human being wouldn't want to save time?

1. **Objection:** 'Sounds interesting, send me a quotation.'

2. **Decode:** 'You appear to be about as much use as a monkey in a cheap suit, so let's validate my assumption and get you to give me the only thing I actually need you for, your price. This way, you can let your sales manager know that his "spray and pray" strategy is being followed, even if it's not working.'

3. **Disarm:** 'I can do that, but I need to know more about exactly what you're looking for and to do that, I need to ask you some more questions first. But let's say I do send you a quotation – what would you do with it?'

Again, this could be viewed as aggressive, but it's totally logical to find out what giving away your price gets you in return. Ask them. If you don't get confirmation that they need it to sign off the funds to approve the deal, why send it? A quotation must be viewed as a formal confirmation that your prospect has agreed to buy from you – strive for that level of commitment and most of the quotations you send will convert into orders.

The common denominator with all of these examples is the need for you to earn the right to be treated as an equal, so think back to what we covered in chapter three (Rapport). For you to provide value to the prospect, you'll also need to hit their 'What's in it for me?' factor (see chapter six, Resource). Combine these two key elements and you'll find that more prospects will want to engage with you and you'll have more control over what happens when you do.

The OBJECT formula

Follow the sales process in this book and the chances of you hearing an objection diminish.

Why? Because you will have engaged with an ideal customer, whose problems you can solve. You'll have controlled the conversation in a respectful and empathetic style, allowing them to uncover their own pain and quantify the size of their problem in both emotional and financial terms. They'll have a sense of urgency and be committed to working collaboratively to ensure that funds are available and all stakeholders on board. Perfect.

Does this mean you won't get objections? Of course not. I still do today, as my earlier example showed. You must be prepared for them to come and know how to help your prospect deal with them successfully when they do. A great framework to use for this is OBJECT, which I encourage you to commit to memory.

Let's take a look at what it is and why it works.

O - Open-minded

Think back to chapter one (Resilience) and the advantage that comes with mastering your mindset. There are many skills that will serve you well, the most important being empathy, being able to put yourself in someone else's shoes. Setting aside any preconceived ideas about why your prospect has raised an objection is not only the right thing to do, it's crucial to being able to help them.

They have one – accept it, acknowledge it and be curious about why you allowed it to manifest and how you're going to build a case for your prospect to help them solve it.

B - Bank

Here's the thing. You and your prospect are 80% through the sales process and if you get over this hurdle, you're home and dry. You've both invested time, effort and resource to get this far and while there's something wrong with the deal currently – hence the objection – there's plenty about the deal that's good. Your next step is to bank the good stuff for two important reasons.

First, by signing off the good elements of the deal, your prospect is reminded of the bigger picture, bringing them confidence that they're with the right supplier. Second, it eliminates the opportunity for the prospect to raise another objection later in the deal.

J – Justify

This is obvious, but rarely applied. Upon hearing an objection, the order-takers out there will go into 'fight or flight' mode. They'll respond to a price objection with either a 'No it's not!' and kill the relationship, or (more typically) respond by unbuckling their belt and lowering their trousers with a 'Would a 10% reduction do it for you?'. Avoid both of these at all costs, they're embarrassing and unnecessary. Simply ask the prospect to confirm why they feel their objection is justified.

You cannot solve a problem that doesn't exist, so ask them to explain. Ask, 'What makes you say that?' and listen to their response. If they can't justify it, it isn't an objection. If they can, you now have evidence that you can work with.

E – Economics

Next, your response must be to validate their objection against the work you did in the previous chapter. Is there a legitimate case for a price objection if your solution saves them five times their investment? Of course, they can 'think it over', but reminding them that every day they put off taking action is costing them money should focus their attention to not spend too long thinking about it.

This is why the Reassure stage of the sales process is so important. Time spent building a business case and assets is time you can usually avoid spending later.

C – Commitment

Again, it's not rocket science – you need the C-word if a sale is going to happen. But it's the part of the job that requires a backbone, not a wishbone. If you don't ask, you don't get. It's that simple. Now is not the time to buckle and negotiate, that's what untrained sales-people end up doing. Remind the prospect that your price is *the* price and that to achieve all the rewards you've identified, it's the price they must pay.

Ask yourself this: if you signal a lower price at this stage of the sale, what does it say about the validity of your original price, your belief in your product and you as a salesperson?

T – Timeout

If you still can't find a way to help your prospect solve their objection and if it's starting to feel like you're both going around in circles, it's time to take a strategic period of reflection. Nothing helps shift emotion to logic quite like an agreed mini-sabbatical, so if it looks like you're stuck in stalemate, tap the brakes, pause, reflect and agree to meet again later. Doing this buys you both time to make the right decisions without unnecessary pressure.

Let's be clear, a timeout is not an indication of weakness or a signal of retreat. Provided you have a clear commitment to meet within forty-eight hours to pick up the conversation, pausing now is a sign of maturity and control.

The key to objections is knowing they exist in the first place, then doing all you can to help your prospect discover that they're concerns at worst and simply questions asking for more information at best. Follow the OBJECT formula and you'll take your prospect on a logical process of discovery and ultimately, reach a conclusion.

Treat these experiences as an opportunity to learn more about yourself as well as your prospect. Why did the objection come? Which part of the sales process was responsible? What did you do or not do that allowed the thought they had to manifest into a concern? What can you learn from it and what can you do differently next time?

What does all this mean for the sales process?

We now know that spending more time at the start of the sales process in the disqualifying phase means that we'll get fewer objections later. There's nothing wrong with hearing 'No' – it's part and parcel of selling – but if we have to hear bad news, we want to hear it at the start, not the end of our process.

Objections will come, but following the sequence in this book all but eliminates them. It also allows us to see objections for what they really are: concerns or requests for more clarity or information.

As with everything related to making good decisions, we have to separate ourselves from the emotion that can cloud our thoughts and create knee-jerk reactions, and shift to logic. Taking time to gather data and get clear on the correct response is what every high-performing sales professional should strive to do.

WHAT'S ONE THING YOU COULD DO TODAY?

List all the objections you hear in your role. Against each, assign the reason why a prospect would say it. Next to this, write down what you must do to avoid the objection from happening. Practise these actions going forward.

---

9 Resolve

Tell me something, have you ever sent a prospect a quotation and it didn't result in a sale?

It wasn't until 2008 that the penny dropped for me about sending out quotations. I was a sales manager working for a large global packaging manufacturer and in my customer portfolio were a number of distributors. These companies bought packaging in bulk from me and sold it on in smaller lot sizes for a premium.

Typically, once a week, they would ask for a price for a certain type and quantity of packaging. It wouldn't be unusual for me to send out more than 200 quotations a year and while I always followed up, very few converted into firm orders. I'm embarrassed to say that back in those days, not only did I not follow the sales process in this book, I also didn't measure the conversion rate of the quotations I spent hours writing, either.

I'm laughing to myself as I write these words and I'm hopeful that you might be, too, because we're this far in the book and we haven't gone into the topic of quotations or proposals until now. Yet the fact that we've managed to help a prospect successfully travel almost 90% of the way along the sales process without needing to is testament to my naivety back in 2008 and underpins the validity of the content in this book.

I remember having another one of those 'How did you get on with the quote?' conversations with my contact at the distributor. My ever-pleasant contact Carol replied, 'Sadly, Matt, our customer thought the price was too expensive compared with their current supplier, so it's a no this time, I'm afraid.'

For those of you into your motivational quotes, you'll no doubt be aware of the belter, 'Insanity: doing the same thing over and over again and expecting different results.' Well, welcome to my mad world back then. While I've since solved the conundrum I had for myself, it brings me no comfort knowing that too many in the sales industry continue to 'spray and pray' their prices around like confetti at a cheap wedding.

But why do they?

Spaghetti throwing

Cards on the table – the act of sending quotations and proposals is an utter nonsense unless you know what you're doing. In the wrong hands, this seemingly essential function can be at best a total waste of your time and at worst, a written legacy of your naivety. However, many organisations operate in a market where documenting 'what's been agreed' between buyer and seller is the correct way to do business. For most, it's expected.

Some sales trainers I know continue to mock the act of quoting. I do not. Every sale I make is based on a formal proposal that always gets signed by the buyer because I mitigate the risks that would stop them doing it. The risks are predictable and obvious when you see them. Let's take a look at a few.

Sending the proposal too early

I'm not talking about speed of response here (I'll cover that next). If the objective of a quotation or proposal is to win business, for that to happen the customer needs to say 'Yes'. If they don't, then there has to be something missing that's stopping them from saying it – correct?

There's a whole raft of things that we include in a quotation, like technical specifications, lead-time, price, payment terms, and terms and conditions, but assuming you've included these and you still get a 'no', what gives?

For me, a quotation or a proposal is simply a confirmation of what's been agreed between the buyer and seller. Until we get a verbal agreement that they want to buy, why would you waste your time sending something that's not complete? For it to be complete, the buyer must have confirmed to you that they want to do business with you and you must have included all of the things they're looking for.

If there's an element of doubt in your mind that the next proposal you send isn't going to result in a sale, I would respectfully suggest that you're sending it without all of the necessary boxes ticked. And that's too early.

Sending the proposal too late

My first, rather brilliant, 'real' sales manager once told me, 'One day older, one day colder' and in the world of sales, that's about as true as it gets. Ask yourself this: as a customer, is there anything more frustrating than waiting for a quotation when you want to buy something? We're so used to the instant online experience these days, that this thing that we used to call 'delighting the customer' is now a formality. The consumer customer expectation meter is off the charts these days, and this is rapidly transferring into the

B2B space, even though these complex sales take just a little more time.

Maybe it's just me, but sending a proposal less than twenty-four hours after being asked could smack of desperation. But with every day that passes, you not only frustrate the buyer with your flippant disregard for time, your nonchalant inactivity signals a benchmark for your future intentions. 'If this is how they operate when they're trying to win our business, what will it be like when we want a delivery?' your prospect thinks as she Googles your competition.

With my sales training clients, I've found that there's a three-day sweet spot between having the final prospect meeting and submitting my proposal. By also confirming the exact time of delivery – and trust me, I do this – the buyer looks forward to receiving it and is reassured by my professionalism.

They don't include the pain

Remember, the buyer is asking you to send a proposal because your product or service addresses their need. When you met the client to discuss this, there was urgency on their part about the importance of solving their problem. But it's only natural that their emotional state will have calmed since you met. It's your job – no, it's your moral duty – to remind them of their pain again now.

If you fail to do this, there's a chance that whatever mood they're in when they read your quotation could influence their next steps and that may not be helpful for you. Consider starting your proposal or quotation with a brief, factual reminder of why they need you – a couple of lines that set the scene and bring back that emotional intensity.

Doing this focuses their thoughts on the value you've brought to them during your sales discussions and provides reassurance before they do what typically happens and head to look for your price.

There's only one option

If, during a moment of weakness, you've ever found yourself gazing at the menu in a fast food outlet, while you were certain walking in that you were having a cheeseburger, why is it the double hamburger that now tickles your fancy? We all like to have choices. These gastronomic options might not do much for the waistline, but they do provide an insight into how offering a choice can help people buy and give you the opportunity to upsell ethically.

In your next quotation, consider providing three options for your solution, for example, 'value', 'standard' and 'premium'. Not only does this show the buyer that you've considered their needs and worked hard to find more than one solution, there's a ton of psychological evidence out there that suggests that when a choice of three exists, the 'standard' and 'premium' options are selected far more than the 'value' option because we're taught to associate premium with quality and reference it against price and value.[10]

There's no guarantee

They know you, they like you and they trust you. Your product or service solves their problem and delivers a return on their investment and they're OK with your terms and conditions and even your price... and yet, they're still not buying – why?

The problem is *you* know your product will work, but they don't. How can they, when they've never bought anything from you before? Their finger is hovering over the 'Buy Now' button as they think to themselves, 'I'm not sure, what happens if it doesn't deliver what they promised?'

By including a guarantee in your quotation or proposal, you'll remove any doubt the buyer may have by taking their risk away and putting it where it should reside – on you. Trust me, nothing helps a twitchy buyer make a purchase more than a risk-reversal clause, called 'Your Guarantee'. If you believe in your product and know it delivers the solution your buyer craves, then why wouldn't you guarantee it?

---

10   https://blog.hubspot.com/sales/the-psychology-of-choice

Price gets quoted for the first time

Sounds weird, because isn't that the point of sending a quotation, confirming to the customer what our price is? Yes, it is, but notice the headline says 'for the first time'. Obviously, we have to include our price, but you want the buyer to receive it as a confirmation of what's been discussed and not a surprise. Not everyone likes surprises.

Why would you waste your valuable time writing a quotation or proposal if you felt they were going to be surprised and then object to your price? If that's going to happen, wouldn't you rather be in front of them to talk it over? I'd advise you to be there to help them reverse their objection and keep the deal alive, exactly as we covered in the last chapter.

Think back also to chapters six and seven (Resource and Reassure): true sales pros establish the buyer's budget and decision-maker status earlier in the sales process during the Resource step and stretch it during the Reassure step.

They only send it by email

OK, I admit it, I do send proposals via email. But it's not my only method for delivery and certainly not my first choice. Nothing beats being face-to-face with a buyer so you can go through the clauses, reassure them of your terms and address any issues on the spot. If logistically this is a challenge, a video call becomes the next best thing.

I also post a hard copy and include a hand-signed letter to 'announce' the proposal. Call me old-fashioned but I still believe that taking the effort to write a letter and deliver a printed document says a lot in today's culture of email-overdose and internet noise. Think about it – most, if not all, letters get opened. Can we say the same about email?

There's no follow-up

In my experience, too many salespeople send a quotation or proposal by email and then wait...

And they wait...

And wait some more...

And wait just a bit longer...

"Ring, goddammit!"

This is great news for the sales novice, because it provides just enough time for them to think of some way to tell the boss that the 'dead cert' deal they promised to land hasn't actually landed yet! Take my advice, never send a quotation until you've called ahead and confirmed a date and time when you can discuss their feedback. Send it without this reciprocal commitment and you'll not only devalue your offer, but you may never get a reply.

Asking for the sale

Back in the day, sales was all about the close. Much of what was served up on the illustrious topic of closing during the era of the great motivational speakers Zig Ziglar,[11] Jim Rohn[12] and Brian Tracy[13] was uncomfortable back then, so it's difficult to even consider it as anything other than bad sales practice today. Any kind of seller-centric behaviour will be about as unwelcome today as a clown at a funeral.

Prospects play a different role now than they did back in the day. For a start, they have almost unlimited access to information. What was hidden years ago isn't today, and this offers prospects a more level playing field for the sales game.

---

11 www.ziglar.com
12 www.jimrohn.com
13 www.briantracy.com

They also look at salespeople differently now. In the past, the salesperson didn't have to work too hard to be seen by prospects as a key part of the sale. Today, prospects rarely need salespeople if they want to buy things. In early 2019, Tesla confirmed that they will only sell cars online in future and others will be sure to follow.[14]

The role of the salesperson is becoming more precarious. But despite this, there is one aspect from the bygone days of 'Always Be Closing' that still holds true. While the outdated closing techniques from the 1980s are deemed obsolete, the principle behind why they were created, ie the need to ask for the business, is very much in vogue – in fact, it's never been out of fashion. So why does asking for the sale seem so daunting?

Salespeople may not ask for the business because:

- They've forgotten their parents' advice. No, not the line about 'peeing in the pool makes the water turn red' but this classic: 'If you don't ask, you don't get.'

- They lack the confidence that comes with knowing what to do when they hear 'No'. Akin to imposter syndrome, the fear of being seen as an order-taker paralyses them.

---

14 www.cnbc.com/2019/02/28/tesla-shifts-sales-to-online-only.html

- They haven't earned the right to ask. Their prospect continues to signal uncertainty and doubt. Even the most inexperienced salesperson knows when it's wrong to ask.

- They don't know how to ask for the sale.

In a complex B2B sale, asking for the sale takes a high degree of professionalism and common courtesy. It also requires the salesperson to display honesty and show accountability to the prospect, to demonstrate they'll own their side of the deal and help the buyer reach their goals.

It might sound something like this: 'Daniel, I'm really grateful for your time today and your advice, honesty and input over the last couple of meetings. Everything in this proposal allows you to achieve the solution you are looking for and I want you to be confident that I will own and deliver my part of that outcome. I'm really comfortable that what we've put together here is the exact solution you need, so unless you have any final questions, are you ready to approve us as your supplier and say yes?'

Today's salesperson must strive to be seen as a strategic partner by anyone looking to buy what they sell. This means adopting a process like the ten 'Rs' in this book and deploying it each and every time they sell. Ideally, your prospect will write their own proposal and close the sale themselves.

What does all this mean for the sales process?

It means that you never have to send another quotation or write another proposal feeling uncertain about whether it will convert to a sale.

It also means that when you do send one, you can now see that it's you, rather than your prospect, who is obliged to make sure something happens afterwards.

Sending the proposal or quotation also signals the conclusion of the selling part of the sales process. When they come back with a 'Yes', you'll have moved the prospect from 'closeable' with a 75% 'likely to buy' status to 'closed' and 100% sold.

Congratulations!

WHAT'S ONE THING YOU COULD DO TODAY?

If you send quotations on a regular basis, take a look at your conversion rate. Find out why those who don't convert aren't buying from you. Then learn from it. Start a record of how many you're sending and converting to measure yourself against.

---

10 Return

You've landed a new customer and you've delivered what you promised. They're delighted with their purchase and thrilled that it looks like it will do what you said it would. A real marriage made in heaven. Now the fun really starts!

While there's a certain sense of achievement that comes with the cut and thrust of winning a new customer, keeping them is the secret to sales success. As my good friend Ed Wells once summed up brilliantly, 'Sales isn't about winning the game, it's about the customer wanting to keep coming back to play it.'

Retaining a customer shouldn't require the same amount of effort, skill and resource as it did to originally find them. And if you can keep them coming back, it will usually result in a greater return on investment, too. For this to happen, there are a number of things we must do before we hand over to our colleagues in customer service.

The act of following up is essential for all customers but is even more vital for new ones. Sending a thank you card within forty-eight hours of purchase might sound a bit old school these days, but if you really want to stand out from your competition, be different.

"Go on, I bet you missed me!"

Follow that up with a face-to-face meeting thirty days later. Top of the agenda will be to check that everything you both agreed has either happened or is on track to happen. This meeting is also the place to see if they have any further questions about their purchase. Upon leaving, book another meeting for three months' time – this one is crucial.

Facts tell, stories sell

Three months down the line and your new customer will be well and truly enjoying the fruits of their purchase. This is your opportunity to become part of the celebration and in doing so, create a legacy for new business, which we'll call a case study.

We know from chapter one (Resilience) that buyers are sceptical of anything that salespeople show them – like a company brochure or testimonials on a website. This is partly driven by their internal 'sales shield' and a desire to not be conned out of their hard-earned cash. It's also because much of the material they're being shown is predicated on the seller and not the buyer.

Most case studies I've read seem to follow the same boring, sugar-coated and predictable format: 'Our customer had a problem, we rocked up and saved the day with our RFJ61X flux capacitator and now the customer thinks we're fab!' Meh! The problem with these vanilla case studies is they fail to capture our attention and take us on a journey that we can relate to and buy into – in short, they only deliver the facts.

But facts just tell. It's stories that *sell* and the secret to good case studies is they tell a story that includes more than problem, solution, applause. Here's the framework for your next case study:

1. **Set the scene.** This is where you describe what the customer's life was like before they had the problem that they came to you with. Imagine those words disappearing up the screen at the start of an epic film and you won't be far away.

2. **Share the problem.** Describe the challenge they faced and the impact it was having on their business. Including facts and figures here will not only amplify their previous issue, it will bring context to the story.

3. **Explain how you met.** This is crucial as readers will not only find out why the customer chose you, but if you were referred to them by someone. Recommendation reinforces your credibility as someone who's good at what they do and can be trusted.

4. **Say what you did.** Here's where you demonstrate your expert problem-solving credentials. Maybe you found that the customer's idea of the problem differed to the actual diagnosis.

5. **Show the impact on life today.** No fanfares, fireworks or flux capacitators here. Just the contrast which shows the improvement from before you got involved to the success they're seeing now. Including quotes from the customer to reinforce how your performance helped them.

You may not be creating case studies for every new customer you win, but doing so supports your retention activity with them and builds an excellent marketing narrative for targeting your Ideal Customer Profile. Make case studies a key part of your outbound strategy. Add them to your website and your LinkedIn profile and, above all, be proud of your achievement.

If you find it difficult to ask for case studies after you've won the business, introduce it into the Reassure phase and then formalise it into your proposal at the Resolve stage. Done this way round, instead of having to ask them if they will do one, you'll remind them that they said they would.

You can make it really easy for your customer to provide one by asking them questions in line with the five-step case study process above, recording their answers and editing them into the written word for their approval. If they're really accommodating, you may find they'll even agree to be filmed and create a video case study. However you do them, finding a way to capture more case studies will pay back significantly more than the time you invest to create them.

Say hello to my little friend

There's no better feeling in sales than when someone calls you up having been referred by one of your customers. No qualifying, no pitching and a receptive buyer who is suggesting they want to buy what you've got – perfect! Yet according to HubSpot, while 83% of customers who had a positive sales experience would be happy to provide an introduction that might lead to a referral, only 29% are ever asked for one.[15] Why?

Some people find asking a customer for a name of someone they know awkward. Like the case study request, asking a satisfied customer for an introduction needs to be an integral part of your ninety-day follow-up meeting agenda. Your request can also follow a simple process of how, when and what to say, which can be incredibly effective.

From the outset, you must get your mindset to a place where you feel you're worthy of receiving an introduction. If you're not convinced you are, no one else will be either. You have to have an attitude that, as a result of the way you transform people's businesses with the service or product you provide, you're justified in receiving one.

Next, you need to flip the typical approach of taking the introduction for your own gains and shift it to giving the gift of an introduction for the provider's benefit. The whole introduction process has to be based on you helping the person providing the name benefit from doing so. It might sound like this:

---

15   https://blog.hubspot.com/sales/sales-statistics

'Glen, knowing me as you now do and enjoying the benefits that have come through working together, if you were to put me in front of someone in your network who you believe would be grateful that you did, who would that person be, and why?'

For this 'give rather than take' approach to happen, you have to have done the hard work in creating a debt of gratitude within your customer, enough for them to want to repay it. Your challenge is to make sure that everything you do in the previous steps of the sale is totally focused on making them feel that way, so that you are certain of a positive response when you ask this question.

Once you've received a name, the process is straightforward. You must ask your customer to seek buy-in for the introduction from their contact by phone first. This is an important step – without it, there's the risk you'll be making a 'cold introduction', and that's not what you want. Having your customer call ahead to ask permission is not only the right thing to do, it massively increases your chances of speaking with their contact, because they've agreed themselves that you can.

Also important is your customer's ability to be able to pitch your pitch. They'll have just a handful of seconds to convince their contact why they think it's worth their time to be introduced to you. You might want to ask them what they'll say before they pick up the phone and make the call. It's in your interests to help them be successful, so help them with their pitch.

Having confirmed the request verbally, your customer will make the introduction by email and copy you in. The text must confirm why your customer is introducing you both, and say that it's simply an introduction to allow you to ask them a few questions over a scheduled call to help the new contact understand the reasons why your customer suggested you should both talk. It should also state that it's *not* designed to be a sales call.

Quite often, these agreements to be introduced can fall through the cracks. While prospecting is a daily task for high-performing sales professionals and will be at the top of our to-do list, introducing salespeople to people they know carries high stakes but low priority. To mitigate the chances of your customer not sending the introduction email, you may decide to write a template email and send it over so they only have to cut, paste, sign and send.

Here's an example of an email sent by one of my clients to introduce me to somebody in his network:

9th April

Hi Patrick,

Great to touch base this morning. As briefly mentioned on the phone, the main reason our sales pipeline is still OK is down to this guy, Matt Sykes (copied). He's been an incredible asset to our business.

He's helped us focus on our sales funnel, the R's (he can tell you more) and also our sales methodology. He's offering a free 30min call with contacts in my network that I think may find it useful and I'm keen to support you as much as possible and so I thought it would be useful for you to talk.

Over to you guys!

Best wishes,
Nathan

The final step now is for you to follow up with an email to the new contact and place your customer in copy so you can close the communication loop and assume control of the conversation. In replying, it's essential that you signal that you've done some research to confirm why you think it's relevant for you, and to offer some value to start to engage with their 'What's in it for me?' factor. Here's my response:

10th April

Hi Patrick – good to meet you.

Always keen to talk to anyone who Nathan knows and thank you Nathan (copied) for the introduction.

I'd be keen to find out more about your company – your website looks really crisp btw.

I'm especially interested to know more about how you diagnose problems for your clients, as that's a big part of my business too.

If you're OK with picking a date/time that suits you, then please click this link through to my calendar and I'll look forward to catching up on Zoom.

Best regards,
Matt

Both case studies and introductions should be viewed as integral elements of the sales process. First, they are available with little effort and can lead to significant reward when used as part of your prospecting strategy.

Second, to 'pick' these low-hanging fruit, you have to earn them and knowing this in advance – picturing the reward for a sale done right – will focus your attention on being the best version of you as you can be all the way through the process. Where focus goes, attention flows.

Let's go round again

The objective at your three-month review is to help your customer buy from you again. Now the hard work of 'know, like and trust' has been done, you must capitalise on that. It's your duty as a sales professional.

Additional sales from existing customers is as much about improving profit margins as it is growing revenue. It's also about creating the highest amount of value possible for your customer. Think about it for a minute – when you first met, they had a problem that brought you together. But it was isolated to that one problem.

Chance are you have a whole range of other products or services that could work for them, which at the time you didn't even consider because they weren't relevant. But now you have time to take a good look at everything going on in the world and establish what else you can help them with, and you can do so without the time pressure you had before.

Let's imagine that at your three-month business review meeting, your customer shares a potential new problem with you because they know you have the solution. This is great news! This is the new world you've created for yourself called 'repeat business', so embrace it and take that easy sale and give them what they need... right?

Well, possibly not. Your job is to create maximum return for your customer and sometimes selling them what they need isn't the same as helping them achieve a larger, more strategic outcome through upselling. Taking the easy sale and not striving to create the maximum return for them is work more aligned to order-takers and that's not you.

Upselling does bring challenges, which is why many avoid doing it. The higher stakes can create a greater risk of failure, result in a lack of certainty and increase the likelihood of a customer not committing to take action. Creating maximum return can also extend the duration of the sales process, as there is more cause for caution and more players are involved.

But, explored in partnership with your newfound friend and justified both logically and strategically, creating the highest value for your customer and, subsequently, the greatest return on their investment is not just the right thing to do, it's the *only* thing to do.

WHAT'S ONE THING YOU COULD DO TODAY?

Get into the habit of asking every prospect who *doesn't* match your Ideal Customer Profile, or the ones who do but you can't qualify in through lack of resource, for an introduction. Think, 'If you don't ask, you don't get.'

Conclusion

This book was written in Spring 2020, at the onset of the Coronavirus pandemic. I watched countless organisations who, a month earlier, were successful and profitable lose almost everything. I also witnessed others who were relatively unsuccessful before see exponential growth simply by being in the right place at the right time with the right product. Both victims of circumstance.

What also became clear to me as I watched close friends and customers become furloughed is just how frightening it is not being in control of your own destiny. We are all salespeople – we're all selling something – and as the world has been challenged by the task of assuming a 'new normal', some may use this time in their lives to choose to take more control of their outcomes.

While not everyone in business may have grasped it before, they must now understand the importance of having a consistent flow of sales, what it feels like when you don't, and why it can never be taken for granted.

That is why I wrote this book. To bring clarity to anyone who wants to take more control over their sales results.

It starts with **resilience** and the huge advantage that developing a constructive mindset and attitude gives you for both your performance and results. Learning how to focus on the things that deliver the best payback guarantees that you'll spend more time on them.

Positioning yourself as the go-to salesperson in your chosen market requires effort, but doing so increases your **reach**. Today's high-performers embrace digital platforms and use them as a way to build meaningful relationships with ideal customers.

Recognising that people buy for their reasons, not yours, allows you to build genuine **rapport** and engage with people on their terms. By accepting that the only conversation that counts is the one going on inside the prospect's head, you find ways to join it.

You now know that most people you meet won't want to buy what you sell. That's why you adopt a 'disqualify first' mindset and introduce a set of **rules** that sets out the agenda for you both to work to. Done respectfully and done well, it's this level of control that progresses a sale.

You also know that people only buy for two reasons: to solve a problem or improve something. This understanding, coupled with your desire to understand more about the **reason** why they need your help, shifts you away from trying to sell to people and towards helping people buy what *they* want.

People need help to buy from you. They need access to a raft of tangible and intangible **resources**, like time, the authority to make decisions and the support and agreement of others involved in the buying decision. Your need to help them become your 'Inside salesperson' is always front of your mind.

Your awareness of the C-word – commitment – is something you never take for granted. You're able to **reassure** your prospect that not only is investing their time and money in your product and service the right thing to do, there's no risk attached with doing so.

But you're also a realist. Despite your new level of sales acumen, you accept that, on occasion, deals don't work out the way you plan. This is where being able to **rectify** a prospect's concerns will allow you to keep more deals alive and convert more sales.

Placing a value on what you offer means you don't give it away by sending out quotations or proposals at the wrong time. It's only when you know you can **resolve** their problem, and they've confirmed that they want you to, that the act of asking them to sign on the line is mutually agreed.

All nine of these steps are critical in the act of converting more leads into sales. But creating customers who **return** to give you more sales and recommend you to people they know is the ultimate aim for every sales professional.

I ask only one thing of you as we end our time together and that's to do something with what you have learned in this book. Knowledge isn't power, it's the doing something with the knowledge that is. If I've inspired you to change how you sell for the better or to improve just one part of your sales process, go for it.

Thank you for taking the time to read *Converted*. I enjoyed writing every word and I wish you success at converting more leads into sales.

Acknowledgements

I feel blessed to be able to do what I do for a living. There is nothing more rewarding than being able to help more people to help people solve problems with their product or service, but I know it isn't possible without the support from others.

I offer a special acknowledgement to Neil Foley, my business coach and business partner in my sales training company, Salescadence. Without his advice, frequent injections of wisdom, humour and straight-talking common sense, this book would still not be completed.

I'm truly grateful to all of my clients. Each of them has helped write this book. But I thank in particular Alan Henry, Lee Barnett, Joe Rahman, Ian Tims, Ian White,

Carole Burman, Charlotte Bate and Nathan Lomax, who have all experienced the training that is encapsulated in this book and whose feedback inspired me to write about it.

I'd also like to thank Rebecca Osbourne for enhancing my words with her wonderful illustrations and, of course, the brilliant Joe Gregory and all of the team at Rethink Press for once again helping me turn my thoughts into an asset.

Finally, I'd especially like to thank my wife, Sue and my son, Oliver for their love, patience and understanding as I wrote this book. This is the second time they've gifted me the space and time to write and I'll always be in debt to them for doing so.

The Author

 Matt Sykes is a sales trainer, author, podcast host and public speaker.

He founded his company Psyko Ltd in 2014 and, following time spent running a franchise in the personal development sector, he founded his sales training business Salescadence, which he runs from offices in Norwich, UK.

His vision is to convert the often unpopular, stereotypical image of salespeople into one where they are recognised for the value they bring to the customers they serve and are seen as a force for good.

Matt has clocked up over twenty years of sales experience across a variety of industries and roles, ranging from global corporate B2B relationship management through to owner/start-up lead generation. It's this far-reaching awareness and understanding of how people buy that allows Matt to guide sales professionals to help more people buy from them in a logical and repeatable way.

His first book, *Sales Glue*, published in 2017, is an introduction to the world of performance psychology and sales, and is an ideal book for someone starting out in sales or someone with solid experience who is looking to enhance their performance with mindset and attitude strategies.

Matt is happiest talking about sales and his podcast, 'The Salescadence Podcast', continues to be extremely popular with the sales community and is a source of valuable free content.

His work takes him into various industry and manufacturing sectors. Much of his time is spent working with sales professionals in the recruitment, packaging and finance sectors.

To get in touch with Matt, visit: www.salescadence.co.uk or email him direct: matt@salescadence.co.uk

Salescadence Competence Audit

Interested to benchmark your current sales acumen against the content within *Converted*?

The Salescadence Competence Audit lists 55 statements specific to each of the ten chapters in this book, which will deliver real clarity around those areas where you're performing well and those which could be better.

Take the Audit and you can register for a free follow-up call with the team at Salescadence, who give you feedback and recommendations based on your results.

This is a great complimentary tool to help you learn more about your sales skills, strengths and weaknesses, and help you shift from good to great.

To take the Salescadence Competence Audit, visit: www.salescadence.co.uk/salescadence-competence-audit